THE
UNIVERSE

Pam Spence
Consultant: Iain Nicolson

HarperCollins*Publishers*

Pam Spence gained an MSc in astronomy at the University of Sussex and worked on a research fellowship in solar physics at the Mullard Space Science Laboratory, University College London, until leaving to become Editor of the popular monthly astronomy magazine, *Astronomy Now*. Now a freelance astronomer and science writer, she continues to be very involved with the amateur astronomical community and is a former President of the Federation of Astronomical Societies.

Iain Nicolson is a writer, lecturer and broadcaster in the fields of astronomy and space science, a Visiting Fellow of the University of Hertfordshire and a Contributing Consultant to the magazine *Astronomy Now*. A frequent contributor to BBC television's *The Sky at Night*, he has written 18 books and hundreds of articles.

HarperCollins *Publishers*
103 Westerhill Road, Bishopbriggs,
Glasgow, G64 2QT
www.collins-gem.com

First published 2001

Reprint 10 9 8 7 6 5 4 3 2 1 0

© The Foundry Creative Media Co. Ltd. 2001

ISBN 0 00 710 143 0

Created and produced by Flame Tree Publishing,
part of The Foundry Creative Media Co. Ltd
Crabtree Hall, Crabtree Lane, London SW6 6TY

Printed in Italy by Amadeus S.p.A.

Contents

Introduction	**6**
How To Use This Book	**8**
PART ONE: The Solar System	**10**
Introduction	10
A Family of Planets	12
Discovering the Planets	14
Asteroids and Meteoroids	16
PART TWO: The Planets	**20**
Diverse Habitats	20
Mercury	22
Venus	28
Mars	34
Martian Moons	40
Jupiter	42
Moons of Jupiter	48
Saturn	50
Moons of Saturn	56
Uranus	58
Neptune	62
Pluto	66
Pluto's Moon	68

PART THREE: Earth   **70**
Our Planet   70
Internal Composition   70
The Earth's Atmosphere   77
Life On Earth   80

PART FOUR: The Moon   **82**
Our Nearest Neighbour   82
The Earth-Moon System   90
The Apollo Moon Landings   94

PART FIVE: Asteroids, Comets and Meteorites   **96**
Space Debris   96
Asteroids   98
Comets   104
Meteorites   110

PART SIX: The Sun   **114**
Our Star   114
Solar Structure   118
Solar Eclipses   124

PART SEVEN: The Stars   **126**
Introduction   126
The Constellations   129
Starlight   130
Stellar Evolution   134
Variable Stars   138

PART EIGHT: Galaxies	**142**
Discovering Galaxies	142
Nebulae	145
The Milky Way	148
Galaxy Types	150
Galaxy Evolution	152
Large-Scale Structure	154
Active Galaxies	156

PART NINE: Understanding the Universe	**160**
Ancient Beliefs	160
Ancient Greek Astronomy	162
Changing Perceptions	164
The Big Bang	170
How It All Works	172

PART TEN: The Future of the Universe	**176**
The Expanding Universe	176
Unanswered Questions	180

PART ELEVEN: Compendium	**182**
Glossary	182
Further Reading and Useful Addresses	186
Index	188

Introduction

OUR HOME planet, Earth, is a tiny speck within the vast Universe. The Universe is everything: there is nothing beyond or outside it, so the study of the Universe is the study of everything. This book explains about the Universe as a whole, and takes a look at the objects that lie within it.

Starting with the Solar System, the book looks at each planet in turn, giving up-to-date information and explaining about the very diverse worlds ranging from the searing heat and poisonous atmosphere of Venus to the icy slush under the surface of Jupiter's moon, Europa. Our own planet, Earth, is looked at in detail, and all other Solar System bodies such as

comets, asteroids and interplanetary debris is examined.

The star within our Solar System, the Sun, is the most studied star in the Universe, and a whole chapter

Earth, the only planet in the Universe known to sustain life.

The Sun is the centre of the Solar System, and the star nearest to Earth.

is devoted to this body. The Sun is a relatively quiet star, and the following chapter reviews the many other types of star that lie in our Galaxy, including black holes, the end points of some massive stars.

The Sun belongs to the Milky Way Galaxy, just one of the many varied galaxies that populate the Universe which are described in a subsequent chapter. The further away a galaxy lies, the further back in time we look. The distances are huge, and because light has taken so long to reach us, we see them as they were millions of years ago.

Learning about the Universe helps us to understand our own world and allows us to observe events and objects that would otherwise remain science fiction.

How To Use This Book

*C*OLLINS GEM UNIVERSE will tell you all you ever wanted to know about the Universe. Divided into 11 sections, it will introduce you to the origin and contents of the Universe to give you a greater understanding of how it all works.

Part One is an introduction to our Solar System, the part of the Universe in which we live. Part Two looks at the eight other planets that exist in our Solar System, and gives essential information about each, as well as looking at their surface features and their moons. Part Three is dedicated to our own planet, and explains why life on Earth is as it is. Part Four is all about the Moon, including its relationship with Earth.

Part Five is concerned with the debris that hurtles through space: what are asteroids, comets and meteorites, and where do they come from? Part Six looks at the Sun, the centre of the Solar System, the celestial body around which the nine planets all rotate.

Part Seven takes a leap further into the Universe to look at the stars, to understand what starlight is and to explain the different types of stars there are. Our galaxy, the Milky Way, is just one of billions of other galaxies, and Part Eight takes a journey into the depths of the Universe to look at what else is out there.

Parts Nine and Ten get to grips with what the Universe is actually about: where it started, how the planets were formed, what is happening now, and what will happen to our Universe in the future. Our changing beliefs about the origins of the Universe and the key figures whose explanations of these questions have shaped our understanding of the Universe are also featured.

Part Eleven is a Compendium containing an invaluable glossary, a list of related books, some useful addresses and an index.

A   B

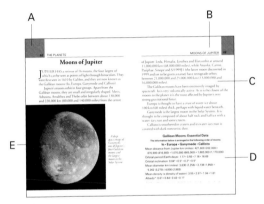

E

C

D

A The page number appears in a colour-coded box, indicating which section you are looking at.

B The aspect of the Universe you are looking at is indicated at the head of the appropriate page.

C The text covers all aspects of the Universe.

D Data boxes on some spreads give useful planetary data or other vital information.

E Photographs and illustrations work with the text to give an all-round view of the Universe and all that is related to it.

The Solar System

Introduction

OUR PLANET Earth is part of the Solar System, at the heart of which is the Sun with 99.86 per cent of all the Solar System's mass. The gravitational field associated with the Sun's mass pulls the rest of the constituents of the Solar System,

Our Sun is both a stable, long-lived, life-giving star and a raging inferno.

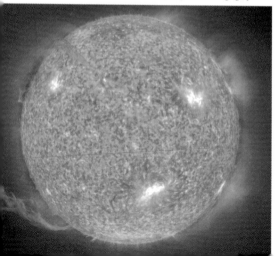

including planet Earth, into orbit about it. The majority of objects lie roughly in the same plane, orbiting the Sun in the same direction.

Mars, as seen from Voyager, is sometimes known as 'the red planet' due to the iron-rich material that forms its surface.

Earth is the third planet from the Sun and is one of four small, rocky, terrestrial planets lying in the inner Solar System. Mercury lies closest to the Sun, then Venus. Beyond Earth is Mars, followed by the gas giants, Jupiter, Saturn, Uranus, then Neptune. Tiny Pluto orbits the Sun and is generally the planet furthest from the Sun, but sometimes its orbit brings it in slightly nearer to the Sun than Neptune.

Earth has one natural satellite: the Moon. The only other terrestrial planet to have moons is Mars, but the gas giants (Jupiter, Saturn, Neptune and Uranus) have complete families while Pluto has just one. The moons of the planets are also diverse worlds in their own right.

Other members of the Solar System include the rocky asteroids that lie mainly between the orbits of Mars and Jupiter, the rocky/icy Kuiper belt objects which lie beyond the orbit of Neptune, and the icy comets which originate in the Oort cloud that surrounds the entire Solar System. These bodies are remnants of material left over from the formation of the Solar System.

A Family of Planets

EARTH IS one of a family of nine planets, the third nearest to the Sun. The inner Solar System has four small rocky planets: Mercury, Venus, Earth and Mars, which are called the terrestrial planets. These terrestrials have thin atmospheres in contrast to the four gas giants: Jupiter, Saturn, Neptune and Uranus, which are predominantly composed of gas and lie in the outer Solar System.

The gas giants are composed primarily of original solar nebula material as they lie too far from the Sun for the gas and dust to have been vaporised like the material in the hotter inner Solar System and they were massive enough to keep hold of these original atmospheres.

The Orbits of the Nine Planets (not to scale)

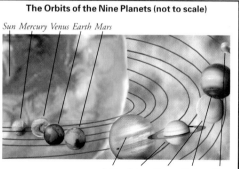

Sun Mercury Venus Earth Mars

Jupiter Saturn Uranus Neptune Pluto
(the Kuiper Belt extends out beyond Neptune's orbit)

Pluto is the smallest planet. It is rocky and icy and generally lies the farthest from the Sun. Sometimes its orbit, which is less circular than that of the other planets, brings it closer to the Sun than Neptune. There has been some discussion as to whether Pluto should strictly be called a planet at all. It is very similar in composition to Triton, the largest moon of Neptune, and both bodies may be objects from the Kuiper belt – the disc of rocky/icy bodies left over from the formation of the Solar System and lying beyond the orbit of Neptune.

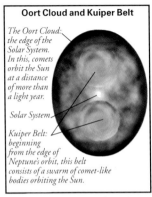

Oort Cloud and Kuiper Belt

The Oort Cloud: the edge of the Solar System. In this, comets orbit the Sun at a distance of more than a light year.

Solar System

Kuiper Belt: beginning from the edge of Neptune's orbit, this belt consists of a swarm of comet-like bodies orbiting the Sun.

OBSERVING THE PLANETS

ONLY FIVE of the planets have been known since antiquity and, even in today's light-polluted modern world, it is possible to see Mercury, Venus, Mars, Jupiter and Saturn with the naked eye. Mercury and Venus lie between Earth and the Sun and are never far from the Sun in the sky. They are observed either in the early evening just after the Sun has set, or early in the morning before the Sun rises. A telescope is normally needed to see the outer gas giants, Uranus and Neptune, and tiny Pluto is very difficult to observe with amateur equipment.

Discovering the Planets

UNTIL 1781, only five naked-eye planets, and Earth, were known. The seventh planet, Uranus, was discovered by William Herschel, a German-born musician who moved to England and became a renowned astronomer.

Herschel first thought the faint fuzzy object was a comet, but it was soon realised it was an object in a roughly circular orbit lying well beyond Saturn. Herschel wanted to call his planet 'Georgium Sidus' after King George III, but it became known instead throughout Europe as Uranus, after the muse of astronomy, Urania, and the name stuck.

By 1830, deviations of Uranus from its predicted orbit suggested to some astronomers that there might be another planet lying beyond Uranus, perturbing it with its gravitational pull. In 1846, the French astronomer, Urbain Le Verrier, published calculations showing where he believed this new planet should be and on 23 September 1846, two astronomers at the Royal Observatory in Berlin, J.G. Galle and H. d'Arrest, located Neptune.

Sir William Herschel, a German-born musician, who turned his interests to astronomy and discovered Uranus.

THE SEARCH FOR PLANET X

IT WAS soon suggested that there might be a further planet beyond Neptune, and the search for 'Planet X' began. Chief among the searchers was the American astronomer, Percival Lowell. Lowell photographed areas of the sky where his calculations led him to believe this planet would lie. In fact, he did photograph Pluto in 1915, but this faint image went unnoticed.

Percival Lowell's calculations re-awakened interest in the search for a planet beyond Neptune.

Lowell died in 1916, but work continued at the Lowell Observatory in Arizona. A special wide-field camera was built and on 18 February 1930, Clyde W. Tombaugh finally found a ninth planet that was very faint and much smaller than Neptune. In a competition, the name Pluto, the mythological god of the underworld, was suggested by Venetia Burney, a schoolgirl from Oxford.

Asteroids and Meteoroids

THE MATERIAL from which the planets formed still pervades the Solar System. This material varies from gas and dust grains to rocky bodies many kilometres across.

Throughout the inner Solar System lie the asteroids (sometimes called minor planets or planetoids). These are rocky, irregularly shaped bodies that range in size from Ceres, the largest of them with a diameter of about 940 km (580 miles) to objects less than 1 km (0.6 miles) across. Smaller items of debris are called meteoroids.

The majority of asteroids lie in the asteroid belt – a region between the orbits of Mars and Jupiter. The distribution of meteoroids is more spread out, but the density is highest near the orbit of Mars.

COMETS

THE MOST spectacular objects in the Solar System are the comets, which can produce awe-inspiring tails millions of kilometres long. Cometary orbits are not confined to the plane of the Solar System, where the planets and asteroids lie, but can approach the Sun from any angle. This fact, together with the number of new comets observed each year, suggests there is a reservoir of cometary material surrounding the Solar System. This reservoir is called the Oort cloud and is believed to extend from around 30,000 to 100,000 astronomical units (AU). An astronomical unit is the mean distance of the Earth from the Sun and is 149,597,870 km (92,955,630 miles).

The Kuiper belt is a second reservoir of cometary material. It extends from about 30 AU out to 100 AU. Cometary material from both the Oort cloud and the Kuiper belt can be deflected by a larger body's gravity into paths that take it in towards the Sun. As it approaches the Sun, the ice in a comet's nucleus sublimates (changes from solid to vapour) to form the basis of the impressive tail.

The Oort cloud has never actually been observed – its existence was suggested by the Dutch astronomer J.H. Oort to explain the trajectories and number of long-period comets (comets that take 200 years or more to orbit the Sun) that are seen. However, comets have been observed coming directly from that far out and it is the logical explanation for their origin.

The comet Hale-Bopp as witnessed in 1997 over Stonehenge.

Comets, such as Halley's comet (pictured), are icy remnants left over from the formation of the outer planets.

THE KUIPER BELT

THE EXISTENCE of the Kuiper belt was also suggested before it was observed. As many of the short-period comets revolve around the Sun in the same plane and in the same direction as the planets, it is probable that they originate within the plane of the Solar System rather than being altered long-period comets which orbit the Sun from every direction.

In August 1992, the first Kuiper belt object was discovered by David Jewitt and Jane Luu, and nearly 100 such objects have been discovered since. It has also been suggested that tiny Pluto and its satellite, Charon, may be Kuiper belt objects, as may

Triton, the largest satellite of Neptune. Triton is an unusual satellite in that it is in a retrograde (backwards) orbit about Neptune and is slowly spiralling in towards its parent planet. This behaviour suggests that it may have originated in the Kuiper belt and been captured by the gravitational field of Neptune.

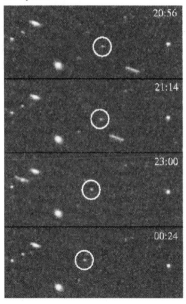

One of the first objects discovered in the Kuiper belt by David Jewitt in 1992.

The Planets

Diverse Habitats

THE WORD 'planet' comes from the Greek word for
wanderer. They are so named because the five naked-eye
planets, Mercury, Venus, Mars, Jupiter and Saturn, can be

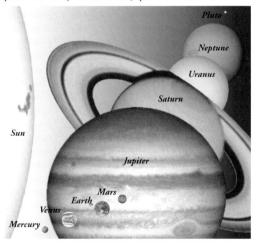

*The comparative size and distance order of the nine planets of the Solar
System in relation to the Sun (not shown to scale).*

seen to meander against the background of the 'fixed' stars. For many centuries astronomers sought to explain the motion of the planets and it was only in the seventeenth century when Johannes Kepler determined that they orbited the Sun in elliptical orbits, that their motion was fully understood.

The inner Solar System contains the terrestrial (Earth-like) planets: Mercury, Venus, Earth and Mars. The terrestrials are relatively small, composed mainly of rocks and metals, and have thin atmospheres. The different atmospheres cause the conditions at the surface of each of the terrestrials to vary considerably. Only Earth, with its vast oceans of liquid water and an atmosphere dominated by oxygen and nitrogen, has conditions suitable for advanced life.

Saturn, with its fantastic rings, is undoubtedly one of the beauties of the Solar System.

The four gas giants, the 'Jovian' (Jupiter-like) planets, Jupiter, Saturn, Uranus and Neptune, are composed mainly of hydrogen and helium. Jupiter is the largest and most massive planet in the Solar System, but even Neptune – the smallest of the four Jovian planets – has a diameter nearly four times that of Earth.

The ninth planet, Pluto, is the smallest. Hovering on the edge of the Solar System accompanied by its moon, Charon, Pluto is a tiny rocky/icy world with a very tenuous atmosphere of methane and nitrogen.

Many of the planets have moons. Earth has just one, but the gas giants have a complete retinue, with each moon displaying a wide variety of surface conditions.

Mercury

T HE INNERMOST planet, Mercury, orbits the Sun in just under 88 days, which explains why the Greeks named it after the fleet-footed messenger of the gods. Never far from the Sun in the sky, Mercury can sometimes be seen shining low in the west immediately after sunset or low in the east shortly before sunrise.

Mercury's surface is heavily cratered, and it has a large core surrounded by a mantle of rock.

STRUCTURE AND COMPOSITION

MERCURY'S MEAN density is similar to that of Earth. It is thought that Mercury contains twice as much iron, by proportion, as any other planet. Its nickel-iron core probably extends out to ¾ of its radius. This core is surrounded by a mantle of rock and a thick crust.

Mercury has a weak magnetic field, about 1 per cent as strong as that of Earth. However, as Mercury rotates so slowly, the magnetic field is unlikely to be created by the rotational movement of a liquid core. It is, in any case, also unlikely that Mercury's core is still liquid as such a small planet would have cooled and solidified long ago. Some astronomers suggest that Mercury's magnetic field is due to some magnetism being 'frozen in' to its solid iron core.

The atmosphere of Mercury is very thin, producing a ground pressure only 2 x 10⁻¹¹ of that of Earth. The most abundant element is oxygen, followed by sodium and hydrogen. There are also atoms of potassium and helium. The hydrogen and helium are captured from the solar wind; the oxygen, sodium and potassium are likely to have been released from rock vaporised during micrometeoroid strikes.

Mercury: Essential Data

Mean distance from the Sun:
  0.387 AU; 57,900,000 km (35,000,000 miles)

Aphelion (point in orbit furthest from Sun):
  69,800,000 km (43,400,000 miles)

Perihelion (point in orbit nearest the Sun):
  46,000,000 km (28,600,000 miles)

Eccentricity of orbit (deviation from circular orbit; 0 = circular):
  0.2056

Orbital period (Earth days): 87.969 days

Axial rotation period (Earth days): 58.646 days

Inclination of axis: 0°

Inclination of orbit to ecliptic (how much the planet is inclined to Earth's orbit): 7°00'16"

Equatorial diameter: 4,878 km (3,031 miles)

Mass: 3.302×10^{23} kg (7.280×10^{23} lbs) (0.055 x Earth mass)

Average density relative to water: 5.4

Surface temperature °C/°F/K(elvin): 350/662/623 (day), -170/-274/103 (night)

Brightest magnitude*: -1.9

Moons: 0

(*For an explanation of magnitude, see page 129)

Mercury takes just 88 days to complete its orbit around the Sun. Mercury can be seen in silhouette as a black dot (below) crossing in front of the Sun.

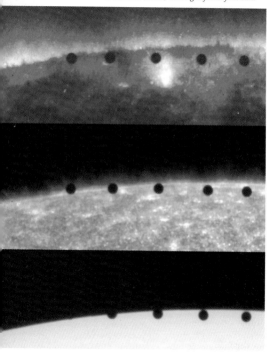

BOTH HOT AND COLD

MERCURY'S SURFACE suffers the most extreme temperature changes of any planet. Its thin atmosphere does not protect the surface from the heat of the Sun, and being the closest planet to the Sun means that its surface temperature can rise to 700K (427°C/800°F). In addition, because of Mercury's slow rotation on its axis and rapid orbital period, nights can last for many months. Thus, on Mercury's night-side, the temperature can drop to 100K (-173°C/-279°F), one of the coldest places in the Solar System.

As Mercury's rotation axis is very nearly perpendicular to the plane of its orbit, there are regions at its poles – on the floors of some craters – that are never exposed to sunlight. Recent radar images have shown bright spots that may be water-ice deposits.

Mercury has a very dark surface and reflects only about 6 per cent of the sunlight it receives.

The Antoniad crater region is just one of many to appear on Mercury's heavily cratered surface.

SURFACE FEATURES

ONLY ONE spacecraft has flown close to Mercury. In 1974 and 1975, Mariner 10 made three fly-bys at a range of 756 km (470 miles) but, because of how it orbited the planet, it was only able to image about 45 per cent of Mercury's surface.

Mercury's surface is heavily cratered and can be divided into the highlands and the lowland plains. The highlands are much more heavily cratered than the lowland plains.

The craters on Mercury are similar in structure to craters seen on the Moon and were mostly created by the impact of meteoroids early in the life of the Solar System. The smaller craters are bowl-shaped; larger craters have flatter interiors with scalloped rims, central peaks and terraces on their inner walls. However, as Mercury's gravity is nearly 2.5 times that of the Moon, material (called ejecta) flung out on impact do not travel so far as on the lunar surface.

The largest impact feature is the Caloris Basin with a diameter of 1,340 km (833 miles), produced about 3,850,000,000 years ago when an object around 150 km (90 miles) across hit Mercury.

The seismic impact travelled right through the planet and fractured the crust on the opposite side. The Basin is surrounded by concentric ridges up to 2 km (1.2 miles) high.

The lowland (or smooth) plains occur within and around the Caloris Basin. These may have been produced by molten magma seeping through the crust.

Mercury has some unique features like the long, sinuous, cliff-like

The Caloris Basin is one of Mercury's most distinctive surface features.

features known as lobate scarps. They range in height from a few hundred metres to 2 km (1.2 miles) and in length from 20 to 500 km (12 to 300 miles). They formed when Mercury cooled and shrank slightly, creating wrinkles in the solidifying magma.

Venus

THIS PLANET is named after the Roman goddess of love. Because it is only slightly smaller than Earth but lies nearer to the Sun, Venus was once thought to be a tropical paradise; in fact it is a tropical hell with searing temperatures, crushing pressures, a poisonous atmosphere and acid rain.

At 41 million km (25 million miles) away at its closest approach, Venus is the nearest planet to Earth. Like Mercury, Venus is never far from the Sun in the early evening or morning skies. Shining brilliantly near the horizon, Venus is often called the evening or morning star and, apart from the Sun and the Moon, is the brightest object in the sky.

As Venus goes around the Sun, its appearance as seen from Earth changes (it goes through phases just like the Moon).

STRUCTURE AND COMPOSITION

THE INTERNAL structure of Venus is probably very similar to Earth's with a nickel–iron core surrounded by a silicate mantle.

Venus has no discernible magnetic field. This may be because it revolves very slowly on its axis, taking just over 243 days to turn 360 degrees, or because it does not have a liquid outer core.

Venus: Essential Data

Mean distance from the Sun: 0.723 AU; 108,200,000 km
  (67,200,000 miles)
Aphelion: 108,900,000 km (67,700,000 miles)
Perihelion: 107,500,000 km (66,800,000 miles)
Eccentricity of orbit: 0.0068
Orbital period (Earth days): 224.70 days
Axial rotation period (Earth days): 243.01 days (retrograde)
Inclination of axis: 177°
Inclination of orbit to ecliptic: 3°23′40″
Equatorial diameter: 12,104 km (7,521 miles)
Mass: 4.869×10^{24} kg (1.073×10^{25} lbs) (0.815 x Earth mass)
Average density relative to water: 5.24
Surface temperature °C/°F/K(elvin):
  480/900/750
Brightest magnitude: -4.4
Known moons: 0

As well as being very slow, Venus's rotation is retrograde – in the opposite direction to the other planets (except Uranus) and opposite to the direction in which it orbits the Sun. One suggested cause is that Venus might have suffered a huge impact during its early history, but no concrete evidence of this has been discovered.

Optimal times for viewing the planet Venus include early morning and twilight (pictured).

A KILLER ATMOSPHERE

VENUS'S ATMOSPHERE is incredibly thick, extending 250 km (155 miles) above the surface, and is 96.5 per cent carbon dioxide with small amounts of nitrogen and traces of other inert gases. The carbon dioxide was produced by the widespread volcanism that Venus suffered in its early history.

Carbon dioxide is a very efficient greenhouse gas; radiation from the Sun reaches the surface of Venus where it is absorbed and re-radiated in the infrared. This infrared radiation is absorbed by the carbon dioxide, heating up the lower atmosphere which re-radiates the energy back to the ground, and so the surface of Venus heats up. The temperature at Venus's surface is a searing 750K (480°C/896°F).

The surface is so hot that any rain (on Venus rain is made of sulphuric acid droplets) is vapourised before it reaches the ground. There is about 30 km (19 miles) of clear dry air above the ground, then haze reaching up to the beginning of the cloud layers at 48 km (30 miles).

The atmospheric pressure on the surface of Venus is a crushing 90 times that of Earth.

The Russian Venera 13 returned the first colour images of Venus's surface (pictured) after penetrating its dense gaseous atmosphere.

The 8 km-(5 mile-) high extinct volcano Maat Mons (pictured), as captured by the Magellan space probe.

SURFACE FEATURES

VENUS'S THICK blanket of cloud stops us seeing any surface features with ordinary telescopes, but 99 per cent of the surface has been mapped using radar techniques.

Volcanic features dominate Venus's surface. Relatively flat volcanic plains cover about 85 per cent of the surface, crossed by meandering lava channels. The longest channel, the Baltis Vallis, runs for 6,800 km (4,200 miles).

Fractures and faults criss-cross the whole of Venus's surface, while other volcanic features include pancake domes (circular, flat-topped domes formed from viscous lava), coronae (large volcanoes surrounded by concentric fractures) and tesserae (long elevated tracks crossed by ridges).

Roughly circular-shaped, shield volcanoes with diameters less than 20 km (12 miles) are common. Volcanoes between

20 and 100 km (12 and 60 miles) in diameter often have
distinctive deposits radiating out from a central vent. Larger
volcanoes such as Maat Mons, which is 8 km (5 miles) high, are
concentrated on the highland regions.

The two main highland areas are called Ishtar Terra and
Aphrodite Terra. Ishtar Terra is in the northern hemisphere and
is bounded on three sides by mountains, including the Maxwell
Montes, the highest mountain range on Venus. Aphrodite Terra
lies mainly in the southern hemisphere.

Venus does not have as many impact craters as the Moon
or Mercury do because early craters have been erased by
volcanic activity.

*Venus's surface is a mixture of highlands, mountains and plains; this is
known as the Eistla Reigion.*

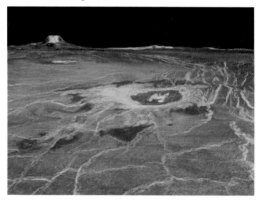

EXPLORING VENUS

THE US Mariner 2 was the first successful fly-by mission to Venus, in 1962; it was followed by Mariner 5 (1967) and Mariner 10 (1974).

The Soviet Venera probes were designed to drop through the atmosphere and land on the surface. Venera 4 transmitted data for 94 minutes as it descended on 18 October 1967, while in May 1969, Veneras 5 and 6

Venus as seen during the day; after the Sun and the Moon, Venus is the brightest object in the sky.

transmitted for 53 and 51 minutes respectively. Venera 7 reached the surface on 15 December 1970 and worked from the ground for 23 minutes; on 22 July 1972, Venera 8 transmitted 50 minutes of data from the surface.

In 1978, two US Pioneer Venus spacecraft were launched. These dropped probes into the atmosphere and mapped about 93 per cent of the surface.

The most recent spacecraft to visit Venus was NASA's Magellan, which reached the planet in 1989 and mapped about 99 per cent of the surface, revealing features as small as 100 km (60 miles) across.

The Venera spacecraft revealed the Venusian surface to be rocky desert. Venera 9 showed sharp angular rocks near the lander, while Venera 10 revealed an older, more eroded region.

Mars

W HEN IT is visible in the night sky, Mars has a noticeable reddish hue. Sometimes called the Red Planet, Mars was named after the Roman god of war.

A composite image of the Martian globe taken by the Hubble Space Telescope (HST).

STRUCTURE AND COMPOSITION

MARS LIES farther out from the Sun than Earth and is only about half the size, with a density similar to that of the Moon. This indicates that Mars's iron core makes up a smaller proportion of its volume than do the cores of the other terrestrial planets and that it might contain large amounts of sulphur. Mars has little discernible magnetic field, but some evidence suggests it may have had one in the past.

Mars's axis of rotation is tilted only slightly more than Earth's to the ecliptic (the plane of Earth's orbit round the Sun). This means that it orbits the Sun at a similar angle as Earth (25 degrees as opposed to 23 degrees) and Mars experiences similar seasons to Earth, although its southern winters are colder and longer than those in its northern hemisphere. Both Martian polar caps have a permanent layer of water ice with seasonal carbon dioxide ice frost; the southern polar cap may retain some of the carbon dioxide ice throughout the Martian year.

The atmosphere is thin and composed mainly of carbon dioxide. Atmospheric pressure is only about one per cent that of Earth; it may have been more in the past, but Mars's lower gravity means it is difficult for it to hold on to a denser atmosphere.

The atmosphere is not thick enough for any effective greenhouse heating to occur. Daytime temperatures rarely rise above 273K (0°C/32°F), and at night they can fall to 133K (-140°C/-220°F).

Mars: Essential Data

Mean distance from the Sun: 1.524 AU; 227,940,000 km (141,640,000 miles)

Aphelion: 249,200,000 km (154,800,000 miles)

Perihelion: 206,600,000 km (128,400,000 miles)

Orbital period (Earth days): 686.98 days

Axial rotation period (Earth days): 24.623 days

Inclination of axis: 25°19′

Inclination of orbit to ecliptic: 1°50′59″

Eccentricity of orbit: 0.0934

Equatorial diameter: 6,794 km (4,222 miles)

Mass: 6.410×10^{23} kg (1.413×10^{24} lbs) (0.107 x Earth mass)

Average density relative to water: 3.9

Surface temperature °C/°F/K(elvin):
   20/70/293 (day), -140/-220/133 (night)

Brightest magnitude: -2.0

Known moons*: 2

(*For more details on Martian moons, see page 40)

SURFACE FEATURES

IT WAS once thought that intelligent beings inhabited Mars – beings who fought against the death of their planet by building canals to irrigate a drying landscape. Mars *is* dry, but no evidence of civilisation has been found – the 'canals' were a trick of the poor optics being used.

The Martian surface can be divided into highlands 1 to 4 km (0.6 to 2.5 miles) above the mean surface level and the lowlands (much of them lying below the mean surface level). The highlands are mostly in the southern hemisphere and are heavily cratered; the lowlands are a younger surface with much less cratering.

Martian impact craters are different to lunar craters; the ejecta around them look like a flow of slurry, which would be consistent with the idea that in the past, water or ice was present in the Martian ground.

Other features, including valleys that resemble dried up river beds, also suggest that water may once have flowed freely on Mars. In 1998 Mars Global Surveyor detected high levels of

Dried-up gullies feature in the Martian landscape – possible evidence of past flowing water?

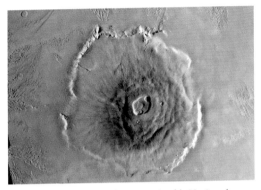

Olympus Mons, the largest and most impressive of the Martian volcanoes.

haematite, a mineral usually produced in iron-rich water heated by volcanic activity.

Mars has much evidence of past volcanic activity, including the largest volcano in the Solar System, Olympus Mons, which rises about 27 km (17 miles) above its surroundings – more than three times as high as Mount Everest. Several large volcanoes occur in the Tharsis region, which is a huge uplift in the crust near the equator. Other volcanoes occur in the Elysium Planitia.

To the east of Tharsis is the Valles Marineris, a vast system of canyons extending about 4,000 km (2,500 miles), reaching up to 600 km (370 miles) wide and 7 km (4 miles) deep in places. The canyons are the result of the faulting and collapse of the Martian surface.

THE RED PLANET

MARS REALLY *is* a red planet. Spacecraft sent to survey and land on the surface have sent back images of a reddish brown, rock-strewn landscape, with a red sky. The colour results from iron-oxide dust, similar to rust, which covers most of the planet.

Huge planet-wide dust storms sometimes rage across the surface. Probably caused by temperature differences between the atmosphere over the retreating polar ice caps and the warmer rocky ground, the storms can obscure the ground for weeks at a time. Suspended dust particles cause the red tinge in the Martian atmosphere.

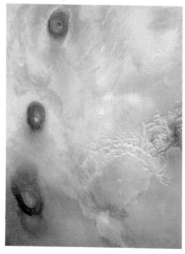

The Tharsis region (pictured) is an upland area on the surface of Mars comprising a chain of three volcanoes.

EXPLORING MARS

THE FIRST mission to Mars was Mariner 4, which flew past in 1965. Mariners 6 and 7 flew past in 1969, while Mariner 9 went into orbit in 1971.

Vikings 1 and 2 reached Mars in 1976; both had an orbiter and lander, and returned data for more than four years. The orbiters photographed the entire Martian surface down to a resolution of a few hundred metres. In 1989, Phobos 2 imaged Mars's moon, Phobos, before communications were lost due to computer malfunction.

A curious image of crater Galle on the surface of Mars which effectively looks like a 'smiley face'.

Other unsuccessful missions were followed by the Pathfinder mission, which dropped a lander to the surface in the Chryse Planitia region on 4 July 1997. On the surface, the rover, Sojourner, explored the immediate vicinity and sampled Martian rocks.

In the same year, Mars Global Surveyor started to study the surface geology and mineralogy, and discovered Mars's weak magnetic field.

Martian Moons

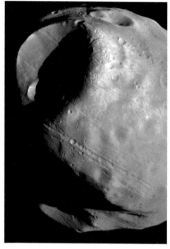

Phobos, the larger of Mars's two moons, has craters on its surface.

MARS HAS two moons: Phobos meaning 'fear' and Deimos meaning 'panic'. Both are small, irregularly shaped objects, and both were discovered in 1877 by Asaph Hall at the US Naval Observatory. It is believed that both are asteroids which have been pulled into orbit around Mars.

Phobos has a large crater, Stickney, which is about 10 km (6 miles) across, and a series of roughly parallel grooves running along one axis. The grooves are deepest and widest near Stickney and may be fractures created during the impact that made the crater.

Phobos orbits around Mars in under eight hours and it will probably impact on the planet in less than 100,000,000 years' time.

Phobos: Essential Data

Mean distance from Mars: 9,270 km (5,760 miles)
Orbital period (Earth hours): 7h 39m
Orbital inclination: 1°4'55"
Mean diameter*: 20 x 23 x 28 km (12 x 14 x 17 miles)

(*As both moons are irregularly shaped bodies, multiple diameters refer to three different axes)

Deimos: Essential Data

Mean distance from Mars: 23,400 km (14,540 miles)
Orbital period (Earth days): 1.26 days
Orbital inclination: 1°47'28"
Mean diameter: 10 x 12 x 16 km (6 x 7 x 10 miles)

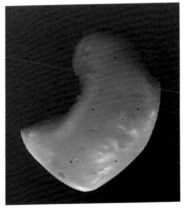

The smaller Martian moon, Deimos, as captured by the Viking planetary probe.

Deimos is much smaller than Phobos and orbits Mars farther out. It has fewer craters than Phobos and many of them appear to be partly or totally filled in with sediment.

Jupiter

JUPITER IS the largest and most massive planet in the Solar System; it has about 2.5 times the mass of all the other planets combined, and its consequentially large gravitational field has an effect on many other bodies in the Solar System. The planet takes its name from the king of the Roman gods.

Jupiter is composed mainly of hydrogen and helium. Different coloured belts and zones can be seen at the cloud tops.

STRUCTURE AND COMPOSITION

JUPITER IS composed mainly of hydrogen and helium. Its huge atmosphere extends about 1,000 km (600 miles), below which lies a region of liquid hydrogen. Pressure and temperatures rise with depth, and at around 25,000 km (16,000 miles) below the outer surface of the atmosphere, the temperature is above 11,000K (10,727°C/19,340°F) with pressure 1,000,000 times that at the surface of Earth. In these conditions, hydrogen becomes a liquid metal and a good conductor of electricity. It is the rapid movement of these liquid hydrogen region that produces Jupiter's strong magnetic field. Jupiter may have a relatively small core of up to about 15 Earth masses composed of iron and silicates.

Telescopes and space probes show the tops of Jupiter's clouds as having distinctive patterns of dark belts and brighter zones. The darker colouration of the belts is thought to result from clouds of ammonium hydrosulphide while the brighter zones have high-level white clouds of ammonia ice crystals.

Jupiter spins rapidly on its axis with a rotational period of under 10 hours. This rapid rotation makes the planet bulge out at the equator and flattens the polar regions. It is also the cause

Jupiter: Essential Data

Mean distance from the Sun:
  5.203 AU; 778,340,000 km (483,640,000 miles)

Aphelion: 816,000,000 km (507,000,000 miles)

Perihelion: 740,600,000 km (460,200,000 miles)

Orbital period (Earth years): 11.86 years

Axial rotation period (equatorial): 9.841 hours

Inclination of axis: 3.08°

Inclination of orbit to ecliptic: 1°18'

Eccentricity of orbit: 0.0484

Equatorial diameter: 142,985 km (88.847 miles)

Mass: 1.899×10^{27} kg (4.187×10^{27} lbs) (317.8 x Earth mass)

Average density relative to water: 1.314

Cloud-top temperature °C/°F/K(elvin):
  -110/-166/163

Brightest magnitude: -2.7

Known moons: 16

of the belts and zones; convection within Jupiter brings material to the cloud tops where the rapid rotation spreads it out in the east to west direction. High wind speeds of 100 m/s (200 mph) or more are found at the boundaries between the belts and zones.

Jupiter radiates about twice as much heat as it receives from the Sun. This energy is probably primordial heat left over from when this giant planet formed, 4,600,000,000 years ago.

Unseen by Earth-bound telescopes is a thin ring system. Discovered by Voyager 1 in 1979, Jupiter's rings are composed of small rocky particles. There are three named rings: the halo ring, the gossamer ring and the main ring.

Although far less conspicuous than Saturn's, Jupiter, too, has its own ring system, probably made of small, rocky particles.

THE GREAT RED SPOT

THE MOST famous marking on Jupiter is the Great Red Spot, the long-lasting weather system in the southern hemisphere. The Great Red Spot is an oval high-pressure anticyclone that has been observed for more than three centuries. Its longevity may be a result of the absence of a solid planetary surface that would cause pressure waves that break up such storms on planets like Earth, or because it absorbs energy from other, smaller storms. The edge of the Great Red Spot rotates anti-clockwise in about four to six days with internal winds of up to 100 m/s (200 mph).

An image from Voyager of Jupiter's Great Red Spot, an eddying cloud system, visible since the nineteenth century.

The Great Red Spot varies in size: at the time of the Voyager fly-bys in 1979, it was the size of Earth; it has also been known to measure up to 40,000 by 14,000 km (25,000 by 70,000 miles). Its red colouration is thought to be caused by traces of phosphorus.

The banded, swirling majesty of the king of all planets, Jupiter.

MAGNETIC AND GRAVITATIONAL EFFECTS

JUPITER HAS a very powerful magnetic field. It is about 20,000 times stronger than Earth's and extends far from the planet, trapping particles emitted from the volcanoes on its innermost Galilean moon, Io. The charged particles remain trapped in a torus (doughnut shape) within Jupiter's magnetic field.

The solar wind buffets against the magnetic field on the sunward side and pulls it out into a magnetotail on the other side. Jupiter's magnetotail stretches at least 650,000,000 km (400,000,000 miles), beyond the orbit of Saturn.

Being so massive, Jupiter has a powerful gravitational field that perturbs passing comets and asteroids. One of the most dramatic effects of Jupiter's gravitational field was seen in July 1994 when comet Shoemaker-Levy 9 was pulled apart into 24 pieces, all of them subsequently colliding with the planet. The impact areas were visible from Earth, even through amateur telescopes.

Jupiter must have pulled many such objects into itself over the aeons, thereby protecting Earth and the other inner Solar System planets from impacts. It is also probably the gravitational tug-of-war between Jupiter and the Sun that stopped another planet forming at about 3 AU, where the majority of asteroids are found, contained in their orbits by the influence of the Sun and Jupiter: the two largest objects in the Solar System.

The aftermath of the impact caused by the comet Shoemaker-Levy 9 on the planet Jupiter.

Moons of Jupiter

JUPITER HAS a retinue of 16 moons, the four largest of which can be seen as points of light through binoculars. They were first seen in 1610 by Galileo, and they are now known as the Galilean moons (Io, Europa, Ganymede and Callisto).

Jupiter's moons orbit in four groups. Apart from the Galilean moons, they are small and irregularly shaped. Metis, Adrastea, Amalthea and Thebe orbit between about 130,000 and 220,000 km (80,000 and 140,000 miles) from the centre

A deep-space image of Ganymede, one of Jupiter's four Galilean moons and the largest moon in the Solar System.

of Jupiter. Leda, Himalia, Lysithea and Elara orbit at around
11,000,000 km (68,000,000 miles), while Ananke, Carme,
Pasiphae, Sinope and S/1999J1 (the latter moon discovered in
1999 and yet to be given a name) have retrograde orbits
between 21,000,000 and 25,000,000 km (13,000,000 and
16,000,000 miles).

The Galilean moons have been extensively imaged by
spacecraft. Io is very volcanically active. As it is the closest of the
moons to the planet it is the most affected by Jupiter's very
strong gravitational force.

Europa is thought to have a crust of water-ice about
100 km (60 miles) thick, perhaps with liquid water beneath.

Ganymede is the largest moon in the Solar System. It is
thought to be composed of about half rock and half ice with a
water-ice crust and some craters.

Callisto is smothered in craters and its water-ice crust is
covered with dark meteoritic dust.

Galilean Moons: Essential Data

The information below is arranged in the following order of moons:

Io • Europa • Ganymede • Callisto

Mean distance from Jupiter km (miles): 421,600 (262,000) •
670,900 (416,900) • 1,070,000 (665,000) • 1,883,000 (1,170,000)

Orbital period (Earth days): 1.77 • 3.55 • 7.16 • 16.69

Orbital inclination: 0.04° • 0.5° • 0.2° • 0.5°

Mean diameter km (miles): 3,630 (2,256) • 3,138 (1,950) •
5,262 (3,270) / 4,800 (2,983)

Mean density (x density of water): 3.55 • 2.97 • 1.94 • 1.81

Albedo*: 0.61 • 0.64 • 0.43 • 0.17

(*Albedo is a measure of reflectivity of an object: 0 being totally black, 1 is totally reflecting)

Saturn

THE SECOND largest planet in the Solar System, Saturn is one of the most aesthetically pleasing with its dramatic ring system visible through amateur telescopes. It is named after the Roman god of the harvest.

About every 15 years, we see Saturn's rings edge-on because of the geometry between Saturn and Earth. The last ring plane crossing occurred in 1995; the next will be in September 2009.

STRUCTURE AND COMPOSITION

SATURN IS smaller than Jupiter, but similar in composition. It is believed to have a small core of rock and silicates surrounded by a 17,000 km (10,000 miles) thick layer of liquid metallic hydrogen. Above this, a 30,000 km (18,000 miles) layer of liquid molecular hydrogen merges with its outer atmosphere.

The colours observed at the cloud tops of Saturn are more muted than those of Jupiter because ammonia condenses at a lower level in the colder Saturnian atmosphere. The muted yellow colour is thought to result from a haze of condensed hydrocarbons suspended above the clouds.

Saturn emits about twice as much energy than it receives from the Sun. Again, like Jupiter, some of this will be primordial heat still being released, but the rest is thought to be

Saturn: Essential Data

Mean distance from the Sun: 9.537 AU; 1,424,000,000 km
  (885,000,000 miles)

Aphelion: 1,506,400,000 km (936,000,000 miles)

Perihelion: 1,347,600,000 km (837,400,000 miles)

Orbital period (Earth days): 29.46 years

Axial rotation period (Earth days): 10.233 hours

Inclination of axis: 26.73°

Inclination of orbit to ecliptic: 2.5°

Eccentricity of orbit: 0.0542

Equatorial diameter: 120,537 km (74,898 miles)

Mass: 5.685×10^{26} kg (1.253×10^{27} lbs) (95.2 x Earth mass)

Average density relative to water: 0.7

Cloud-top temperature °C/°F/K(elvin):
  -180/-212/93

Brightest magnitude: -0.3

Known moons: 22

created as helium droplets fall through the atmosphere. It has been observed that, by proportion, Saturn has less than half the amount of helium in its atmosphere than Jupiter – an observation that fits in well with this hypothesis.

Saturn's clouds create a striated pattern of bright belts and dark zones, similar to those of Jupiter.

A Hubble Space Telescope (HST) image of the rare white spot on Saturn.

Saturn has weather systems similar to Jupiter with long-lived oval spots, although nothing to compare with Jupiter's Great Red Spot. Saturn occasionally has eruptions of bright clouds, probably ammonia crystals condensing out in an upwelling of warm air. These eruptions occur roughly every 30 years – during summer in Saturn's northern hemisphere. Saturn also has belts and zones with associated alternating east and west winds.

Saturn rotates in just over 10 hours, causing significant flattening at the poles. It has faster wind speeds in its outer atmosphere than Jupiter; at its equator, speeds of 500 m/s (1,000 mph) have been observed.

Saturn's magnetic field is much weaker than Jupiter's. Being smaller and less dense (it is the least dense planet in the Solar System), astronomers think that it has a smaller liquid metallic core, and thus a smaller magnetic field.

MAGNIFICENT RINGS

SATURN'S RING system dominates the visual appearance of the planet. Composed of a myriad of independently orbiting particles mainly of water-ice, from grains to objects tens of metres across, they extend outwards for more than twice the radius of Saturn. The ring system has a diameter of 270,000 km (167,778 miles), but a thickness of only a few tens of metres.

*A spectacular false-colour image of Saturn's best known feature:
its ring system.*

Saturn has three main rings: A, B and C, within which most particles are between 1 cm and 5-10 m in size. A and B are separated by the Cassini division, which was first noticed in 1675. The Cassini division is thought to be caused by the gravitational effect of Saturn's moon, Mimas. The division is a gap of nearly 5,000 km (3,000 miles), and close scrutiny by

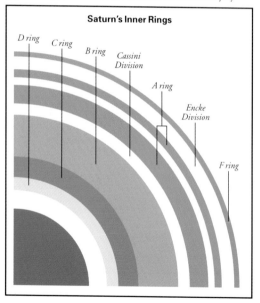

Saturn's Inner Rings

D ring

C ring

B ring

Cassini Division

A ring

Encke Division

F ring

Voyager 1 shows that it is filled with fine particles and several faint rings.

The A ring contains a large number of ringlets and gaps including the 325 km- (200 mile-) wide Encke division, which is observable through some amateur telescopes.

The B ring is the brightest. Crossing the central part of this ring are 'spokes': these 2,000 km- (1,200 mile-) wide dark areas, where a plasma of particles is lifted out of the ring's plane by magnetic fields, radiate out for 10,000 km (6,000 miles).

The C, or crêpe, ring lies inside the B ring. It has a grooved appearance and is made up of many ringlets. In 1980, Voyager 1 noticed a few, widely spaced ringlets extending half-way to Saturn from the inner edge of ring C. They make up the D ring and consist mainly of microscopic particles.

The E ring (not pictured) is also very tenuous. It lies well beyond ring A, and is only noticeable when the rings are seen edge-on. The density of material in the E ring is greatest near the moon Enceladus, and the moon may be the source of material for the E ring, shedding material from meteoroid impacts.

The F ring was discovered by Pioneer II in 1979. Lying just beyond the A ring, F is very fine and consists primarily of dust. When imaged in detail, it was discovered to be several very narrow bands twisted together. Two small moons 'shepherd' the F ring: Prometheus and Pandora. Prometheus orbits Saturn just inside the F ring while Pandora lies just outside. The gravitational perturbations of these two moons keep the icy dust grains contained in their rings.

The most recent ring to be discovered, the G ring (not pictured), is very narrow – about 8,000 km (5,000 miles) wide – and located about 2.8 times the radius of Saturn from the planet itself. It was discovered by the Voyager spacecraft in 1981.

Moons of Saturn

SATURN HAS 22 known moons. Most of these are small and embedded in the rings.

Saturn's largest moon, Titan, was discovered in 1655 by Christian Huygens. The second largest moon in the Solar System, it is the only one to have an

Saturn's largest moon, Titan, is the Solar System's second largest.

Saturn's five largest moons: Essential Data

The information below is arranged in the following order of moons:

Tethys • Dione • Rhea • Titan • Iapetus

Mean distance from Saturn x 1,000 km): 294,700 • 377, 500 • 527,000 • 1,222,000 • 3,561,000

(x 1000 miles): 183,100 • 234,600 • 327,500 • 759,300 • 2,213,000

Orbital period (Earth days): 1.89 • 2.74 • 4.52 • 15.95 • 79.33

Orbital inclination: 1.86° • 0.02° • 0.35° • 0.33° • 14.72°

Mean diameter (km): 1,072 x 1,056 x 1,052* • 1,120 • 1,528 • 5, 150 • 1,436

Mean diameter (miles): 666 x 656 x 654 • 656 • 949 • 3,200 • 892

Average density relative to water: 1.21 • 1.43 • 1.33 • 1.88 • 1.21

Albedo: 0.9 • 0.7 • 0.7 • 0.2 • 0.5–0.05

(*Tethys is an irregularly shaped body, therefore dimensions of three axes are given)

appreciable atmosphere (predominantly nitrogen with traces of hydrocarbons). Due to reach Saturn in 2004, the Huygens probe on board the Cassini spacecraft has been launched to investigate what lies below Titan's clouds. It is thought that there may be lakes of liquid methane on the moon's surface, a source of the methane detected in the atmosphere.

The rest of Saturn's moons can be split into two groups: the small and irregularly shaped, and the icy intermediate-sized. There are 10 named small moons. Six influence the ring system including Pan and Atlas which help create the Encke division in the A ring. Phoebe is the

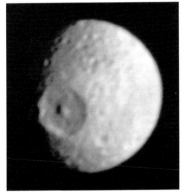

Mimas's crusty surface is believed to have thrown off debris, adding to Saturn's rings.

remotest of the moons and orbits Saturn at a distance of more than 12,000,000 km (7,000,000 miles).

The intermediate-sized group includes Mimas, Enceladus, Tethys, Dione, Rhea and Iapetus. Rhea is the largest of this group and is heavily cratered. Iapetus is unusual with a dark leading edge and a bright trailing hemisphere.

Uranus

URANUS WAS the first planet to be discovered telescopically. It was discovered on 13 March 1781 by William Herschel, and is named after the muse of astronomy, Urania. Subsequently it was realised that Uranus had been seen by others before its discovery, but it had been mistaken for a faint star. It has been found on star charts dating from as long ago as 1690.

The planet Uranus is a cold gas giant.

Uranus: Essential Data

Mean distance from the Sun: 19.19 AU; 2,869,600,000 km
(1,783,100,000 miles)

Aphelion: 3,005,200,000 km (1,867,300,000 miles)

Perihelion: 2,734,000,000 km (1,698,800,000 miles)

Orbital period (Earth years): 84.01 years

Axial rotation period (internal): 17.24 hours

Inclination of axis: 97.86°

Inclination of orbit to ecliptic: 0.773°

Eccentricity of orbit: 0.0472

Equatorial diameter: 51,118 km (31,763 miles)

Mass: 8.683×10^{25} kg (1.914×10^{26} lbs) (14.5 x Earth mass)

Average density relative to water: 1.3

Cloud-top temperature °C/°F/K(elvin): -216/-357/57

Brightest magnitude: +5.6

Known moons: 17

STRUCTURE AND COMPOSITION

URANUS ORBITS twice as far away from the Sun as Saturn. It is the least massive of the four Jovian planets, larger but less dense than Neptune, and less than half the size of Saturn.

Images show a rather featureless disc: the top of a mainly hydrogen atmosphere with some helium and traces of methane. Methane absorbs red light to give Uranus its faintly blue tinge. The atmosphere is not as extensive as Jupiter's or Saturn's, extending down only about 5,000 km (3,000 miles). The planet may possibly have a rocky core (about the size of Earth) surrounded by semi-liquid ices of water, methane and ammonia, or the icy slush may extend all the way to the centre.

SIDEWAYS TUMBLE

THE MOST unusual feature of Uranus is the way it orbits the Sun – on its side. Its axis of rotation lies at almost 98 degrees to the ecliptic. This, coupled with its orbital period of over 84 years, means that each pole alternates between 42 years of continual sunshine and 42 years of darkness.

Despite this, Uranus exhibits extremely faint weather bands and zones similar to Jupiter and Saturn, although there must exist a method of transporting energy from the poles to the equatorial regions.

Uranus has a magnetic field about 50 times that of Earth's. It is tipped at about 59 degrees to its spin axis, which means that its magnetosphere (see page 79 for explanation) interacts with the solar wind in a similar manner to that of other planets.

RINGS AND MOONS

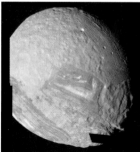

URANUS HAS a system of about 11 thin rings with other broader ring structures. Its retinue of at least 17 moons lies outside the ring system, except for Cordelia and Ophelia which shepherd the outer ring, Epsilon.

The five largest moons were discovered telescopically, while all the others were discovered by Voyager.

Miranda, the smallest of Uranus's moons, was apparently blasted apart and reformed.

The complex terrain of Ariel, as seen by Voyager 2, reveals fault-ridden valleys.

Uranus's five largest moons: Essential Data

The information below is arranged in the following order of moons:

Miranda • Ariel • Umbriel • Titania • Oberon

Mean distance from Uranus km (miles): 129,400 (80,400) •
191,000 (119,000) • 266,000 (165,000) • 435,900 (270,900) •
582,500 (362,000)

Orbital period (Earth days): 1.413 • 2.520 • 4.144 • 8.706 • 13.46

Orbital inclination: 4.22° • 0.31° • 0.36° • 0.14° • 0.10°

Mean diameter km (miles): 480 (298) • 1,158 (720) • 1,172 (728) •
5,150 (3,200) • 1,524 (947)

Average density relative to water: 1.2 • 1.6 • 1.4 • 1.6 • 1.5

Albedo: 0.27 • 0.35 • 0.19 • 0.28 • 0.24

Neptune

NAMED AFTER the Roman god of the sea, and the smallest of the four Jovian planets, Neptune takes more than 150 years to orbit the Sun at a distance of nearly 4,500,000,000 km (2,800,000,000 miles).

STRUCTURE AND COMPOSITION

NEPTUNE IS the densest of the Jovian planets and similar in structure and composition to Uranus. Its atmosphere is primarily hydrogen, with some helium and traces of methane giving it its blue appearance. Like Uranus its interior is predominantly made up of ices.

Neptune's magnetic field is tilted to its rotational axis by 47 degrees and is offset from the centre by about half of Neptune's radius. This suggests that, like Uranus', it originates within the slushy ice interior.

Voyager's close encounter with Neptune showed more prominent cloud

Up until 1989, Neptune's most distinctive marking was the Great Dark Spot (bottom left of image).

Neptune: Essential Data

Mean distance from the Sun: 30.07 AU; 4,498,300,000 km
(2,795,100,000 miles)

Aphelion: 4,535,200,000 km (2,818,000,000 miles)

Perihelion: 4,458,000,000 km (2,770,000,000 miles)

Orbital period (Earth years): 164.8 years

Axial rotation period (internal): 16.11 hours

Inclination of axis: 29.56°

Inclination of orbit to ecliptic: 1.77°

Eccentricity of orbit: 0.0086

Equatorial diameter: 49,528 km (30,775 miles)

Mass: 1.024×10^{26} kg (2.258×10^{26} lbs) (17.2 x Earth mass)

Average density relative to water: 1.76

Cloud-top temperature °C/°F/K(elvin): -216/-357/50

Brightest magnitude: +7.7

Known moons: 8

features than bland Uranus. At the far reaches of the Solar System, Neptune's weather systems are driven more by internal energy than sunlight. Neptune radiates over 2.5 times as much heat as it receives from the Sun, and it is this heat that drives its weather systems.

The most famous marking was the Great Dark Spot but, unlike Jupiter's Great Red Spot, the Great Dark Spot was not long-lasting and had disappeared by 1989.

Neptune has very high wind speeds at its cloud tops – winds of over 500 m/s (1,000 mph) blow parallel to its equator. The winds do not follow the east to west pattern of Jupiter and Saturn and, unusually, at the equator, the winds blow in the opposite direction to Neptune's rotation.

RINGS AND MOONS

NEPTUNE'S RING system was discovered by Voyager 2 in 1989. It consists of six rings (some thin, some broad) with irregular, 'clumpy' rings of varying brightness. Neptune's smaller moons lie within the ring system. Galatea lies within the Adams ring, while Despina, Thalassa and Naiad lie between the Le Verrier and Galle rings.

Triton, the largest moon of Neptune, is probably a captured Kuiper belt object.

Neptune's largest moon, Triton, is larger than Pluto and has the next thickest atmosphere for a moon after Titan. Triton's atmosphere is composed mainly of nitrogen with traces of methane. Triton's surface appears to be covered by solid nitrogen with small quantities of methane, carbon monoxide and carbon dioxide. Voyager images reveal evidence of geysers spewing dark material up to 8 km (5 miles) into the atmosphere.

Triton travels in a retrograde orbit about Neptune, and is slowly spiralling inwards. This suggests it may have been captured by Neptune, rather than have formed close by. Another of Neptune's moons, Nereid, also has a highly elliptical orbit; both moons may be captured Kuiper belt objects.

Neptune's four largest moons: Essential Data

The information below is arranged in the following order of moons:

Larissa • Proteus • Triton • Nereid

Mean distance from Neptune km (miles): 73,548 (45,701) • 117,647 (73,102) • 354,800 (220,462) • 5,513,000 (3,425,613)

Orbital period (Earth days): 0.555 • 1.122 • 5.877 (retrograde) • 360.14

Orbital inclination: 0.2° • 0.6° • 157.4° • 27.2°

Mean diameter: km (miles): 208 x 178* (129 x 111) • 436 x 402* (271 x 250) • 2,705 (1,681) • 340 (211)

Average density relative to water: – • – • 2.06 • –

Albedo: 0.05 • 0.06 • 0.7 • 0.4

(*Larissa and Triton are irregularly shaped, therefore dimensions of two axes are given for each)

Like the other gas giants, Neptune also has a ring system.

Pluto

THE SMALLEST planet, Pluto, hovers at the outer edge of the Solar System although, with its eccentric orbit, it does sometimes approach closer to the Sun than Neptune. There is no possibility of the two planets colliding. Not only are their orbital planes inclined to each other, but when the planets are on the same side of the Sun, Pluto is always well out of Neptune's orbit. Pluto is named after the mythological god of the Underworld.

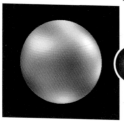

Pluto as seen through the Hubble Space Telescope (right) and (left) a computer-enhanced image.

STRUCTURE AND COMPOSITION

PLUTO IS composed of rock and ice. Its surface is covered by methane and nitrogen ice with traces of frozen carbon monoxide and water. No spacecraft has passed close to Pluto, and Earth-bound telescopes do not reveal much data, but its surface appears to be a patchwork of light and dark areas. The dark areas appear reddish; the lighter patches are probably bright nitrogen ice.

Pluto is very similar in size and composition to Neptune's moon, Triton. They have comparable densities, surface compositions and temperatures, and when Pluto is near perihelion, they are at similar distances from the Sun. All this suggests that Pluto is a Kuiper belt object like Triton, rather than a planet. Pluto will not lose its planetary status, but it has been generally accepted as one of the larger members of the Kuiper belt.

A deep-field Hubble Space Telescope image of the surface of Pluto.

Pluto: Essential Data

Mean distance from the Sun: 39.48 AU; 5,913,520,000 km (3,674,500,000 miles)

Aphelion: 7,381,200,000 km (4,586,500,000 miles)

Perihelion: 4,445,800,000 km (2,762,500,000 miles)

Orbital period (Earth years): 248.54 years

Axial rotational period: 6.3872 days

Inclination of axis: 118°

Inclination of orbit to ecliptic: 17.148°

Eccentricity of orbit: 0.2488

Equatorial diameter: 2,320 km (1,440 miles)

Mass: 1.25×10^{22} kg (2.76×10^{22} lbs) (0.003 x Earth mass)

Average density relative to water: 2.1

Surface temperature °C/°F/K(elvin): -223/-369/50

Brightest magnitude: +13.8

Known satellites: 1

Pluto's Moon

PLUTO'S MOON, Charon, was discovered on 22 June 1978. Astronomer James Christy was working on astrometric plates – measuring the position of Pluto – when he noticed that Pluto seemed elongated in some of the plates, as if it was merged with a faint star. The faint star turned out to be a body almost half the diameter of Pluto.

Charon, named after the mythological boatman who ferried souls across the river Styx, orbits Pluto less than 20,000 km (13,000 miles) from the planet's centre in a period of just over six days. This orbital period is the same as the time it takes both Pluto and Charon to revolve on their axes. Thus they always have the same hemisphere turned towards each other and Charon always hangs over the same part of Pluto's surface.

Pluto's orbit and that of Charon, its moon, are intimately locked together.

Charon: Essential Data

Mean distance from Pluto: 19,640 km (12,204 miles)

Orbital period (Earth days): 6.387

Orbital inclination: 98.80°

Mean diameter: 1,200 km (746 miles)

Average density relative to water: 2

Albedo: 0.5

Charon appears to move north–south in the sky as observed from Earth. This implies that Pluto's axis of rotation is tilted to the ecliptic in a similar manner to Uranus, with Charon passing in and out of the orbital plane of Pluto.

In 1987, Charon was seen to pass directly behind and in front of Pluto, allowing astronomers to deduce a great deal about the orbital characteristics of this very remote pair.

Clyde Tombaugh, the American astronomer who discovered Pluto in February 1930.

Earth

Our Planet

EARTH, OUR home planet, is the third nearest to the Sun. Viewed from space it has a deep blue appearance with wispy, changing cloud cover. The blue colour comes from the liquid water oceans that cover more than 70 per cent of Earth's surface. The existence of these oceans has a profound effect on the planet and the life that inhabits this world.

When viewed from outer space, planet Earth appears blue with a decoratively wispy cloud cover.

Earth: Essential Data

Mean distance from the Sun:
   1 AU; 149,600,000 km (93,000,000 miles)
Aphelion: 152,100,000 km (94,500,000 miles)
Perihelion: 147,100,000 km (91,400,000 miles)
Orbital period (Earth days): 365.256 days
Axial rotation period (Earth days): 23.934 hours
Inclination of axis: 23.45°
Inclination of orbit to ecliptic: 0°
Eccentricity of orbit: 0.0167
Equatorial diameter: 12,756 km (7,926 miles)
Mass: 5.9742×10^{24} kg (1.3171×10^{25} lbs)
Average density relative to water: 5.52
Surface temperature °C/°F/K(elvin): 20/70/293
Known moons: 1

Internal Composition

L IKE THE other terrestrial planets, Earth has a solid inner core. This inner core is mainly iron with some nickel and has a depth of just over 1,200 km (740 miles). Surrounding this is the 2,200 km- (1,400 mile-) deep molten outer core – slightly less dense than pure molten iron so it must contain about 10 per cent of other lighter elements like sulphur or even oxygen. The core is the densest part of Earth and contains about a third of Earth's mass.

Above the core is the transition zone: a 200 to 300 km- (120 to 190 mile-) thick layer called "D". This "D" layer differs chemically from both the core and mantle, and may be either material that was once dissolved in the core, or material that sank through the mantle when Earth was forming.

The 2,200 km- (1,400 mile-) thick lower mantle contains nearly 50 per cent of Earth's mass and is composed mainly of the basalts, silicon and magnesium, and oxygen. It probably also contains some iron, calcium and aluminium.

The 200 km- (120 mile-) thick transition layer, composed mainly of calcium and aluminium, separates the lower and upper mantles. The upper mantle is around 400 km (250 miles) thick and contains refractory materials like olivine and pyroxene which crystallise at high temperatures.

The outer layer, the crust, is composed of low density minerals like silicon oxide and varies in thickness from the 10 km- (6 mile-) thick oceanic crust to the 50 km- (30 mile-) thick continental crust.

Volcanoes occur where two plates move apart; at 4,850 m (1,600 ft) Mt. Kliuchevskaya Sopka in Siberia is one of the world's tallest active volcanoes.

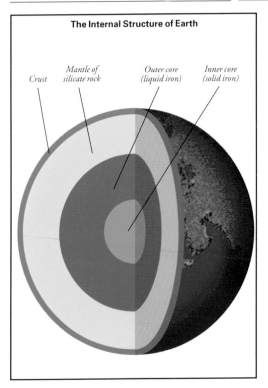

The Internal Structure of Earth

Crust

Mantle of silicate rock

Outer core (liquid iron)

Inner core (solid iron)

PLATE TECTONICS

TOGETHER THE crust and the top part of the mantle make up the lithosphere, a rigid shell about 100 to 200 km (60 to 120 miles) thick. This shell is broken up into a number of plates that move relative to each other at the rate of a few centimetres per year, causing 'continental drift'. About 180,000,000 years ago, all the continents sat together in a single supercontinent called Pangea.

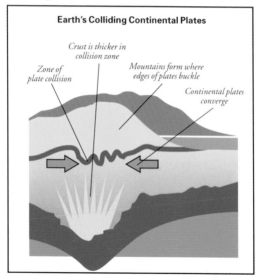

Earth's Colliding Continental Plates

Crust is thicker in collision zone

Zone of plate collision

Mountains form where edges of plates buckle

Continental plates converge

These mountains in Morocco formed when two continental plates collided.

There are three types of plate boundary: diverging, where plates move away from each other; converging, where plates meet head on and one is drawn under the other; and conservative, where plates slide past each other. Earthquakes occur at the boundaries of the plates – rock masses do not slide smoothly past each other and the energy produced shakes Earth's surface. Earthquakes are most common along conservative boundaries and tend to be stronger along convergent boundaries.

Where two continental plates collide, mountain ranges form by the buckling of the edges. Where plates diverge, material from within the mantle is drawn up to fill the space between, forming new oceanic crust. This material can be drawn up in a violent volcanic eruption: such as seen in Iceland.

Volcanoes can also occur at convergent boundaries when the crust of the plate being dragged down, heats up and melts, as in the Andes. Some volcanoes, like those that created the islands of Hawaii, are far from plate boundaries. They lie over 'hot spots' where there is an upwelling in the mantle. This hot-spot volcanism is also the cause of volcanoes on Venus and Mars; Earth is the only planet known to have a plate structure.

A YOUNG SURFACE

THE SURFACE of Earth is continually being renewed by the processes involved in plate tectonics. This is one reason why so few impact craters are seen on Earth. The oceanic crust, for example, only lasts around 200,000,000 years before being destroyed at a convergent plate boundary. Craters are also obliterated by erosion, or buried beneath sediment.

One of the most famous craters is Barringer (or Meteor) Crater in Arizona, USA. It is well preserved because it is in a dry area and relatively young – it was made only about 50,000 years ago.

Many craters are only visible from space. Chicxulub, a 200 km- (120 mile-) wide crater formed about 65,000,000 years ago, is buried under several hundred metres of sediment in Mexico. This crater is the evidence of a massive impact that may have caused the extinction of the dinosaurs.

Meteor Crater in Arizona, one of the best-preserved craters on Earth.

Earth's Atmosphere

EARTH HAS an atmosphere significantly different from the other terrestrials, even though they are formed from similar materials. Nitrogen is the most abundant gas in Earth's atmosphere with 21 per cent oxygen and small amounts of water vapour, argon and carbon dioxide.

All the original atmospheres of the terrestrials were blown away by a strong solar wind (the outflow of material from the Sun) in the early Solar System, and their secondary atmospheres were produced by volcanism and from impacts by comets and planetesimals (bodies that range in size from less than a millimetre to many kilometres that formed the planets by merging together through impacts). Earth's liquid water absorbed much of the carbon dioxide produced in the early atmosphere, and as soon as life forms such as plankton appeared in the oceans, more carbon dioxide was removed by photosynthesis, releasing oxygen.

Earth's atmosphere extends for over 500 km (300 miles), but it becomes so tenuous after even only about 10 km (6 miles), that it is unbreathable for humans. The thin, 12 km- (7 mile-) thick layer closest to Earth's surface is the troposphere, and it is within this layer that the majority of Earth's weather occurs.

Although Earth does not have huge amounts of carbon dioxide in its atmosphere like Venus, the amount of water vapour and carbon dioxide present is sufficient to cause some greenhouse effect, making the surface 30°C (54°F) warmer than it would be otherwise – an amount very critical for life on Earth.

Layers of Earth's Atmosphere

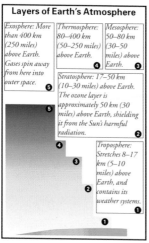

Exosphere: More than 400 km (250 miles) above Earth. Gases spin away from here into outer space.

6

Thermosphere: 80–400 km (50–250 miles) above Earth.

4

Mesosphere: 50–80 km (30–50 miles) above Earth.

3

Stratosphere: 17–50 km (10–30 miles) above Earth. The ozone layer is approximately 50 km (30 miles) above Earth, shielding it from the Sun's harmful radiation.

2

Troposphere: Stretches 8–17 km (5–10 miles) above Earth, and contains its weather systems.

6

5

4

3

2

1

WEATHER AND SEASONS

EARTH'S WARM surface heats the troposphere, which becomes turbulent. Temperatures of 290K (17°C/63°F) at the surface fall to about 220K (-53°C/-63°F) at the top of the troposphere. Warm, moist air rises and cools; the water condenses, forming clouds of water droplets or crystals, creating rain, hail and snow.

Earth's axis of rotation is tilted to the ecliptic by just over 23 degrees. This tilt causes the seasons; when a hemisphere is pointed away from the Sun, it receives less sunlight and the sunlight it does receive falls at such an angle that it has to penetrate more atmosphere to reach the ground. This is winter for that hemisphere. Conversely during summer, a hemisphere receives more hours of sunlight directed through a shorter column of air because of being tilted towards the Sun.

Earth's orbit is not entirely circular and, in fact, during the northern hemisphere's winter, Earth is nearer to the Sun than during its summer. However, the eccentricity of the orbit is minor, and the nearer distance has less effect than Earth's tilt.

MAGNETIC FIELD

EARTH ROTATES once on its axis in just under 24 hours, causing the liquid iron outer core to act like a dynamo and create a magnetic field. Earth's magnetic field is offset from its rotational axis by about 11degrees.

The magnetic field protects Earth from the solar wind. The charged particles of the solar wind are deflected by Earth's magnetic field, creating the magnetosphere. Some particles are trapped within the magnetosphere in two tori called the Van Allen belts.

Other charged particles spiral down Earth's magnetic field lines at the poles. The particles react with the upper atmosphere creating the aurorae or northern and southern lights.

The Aurora Borealis phenomenon (Northern Lights): curtains of light caused by particles of ionised gas from the Sun hitting Earth's atmosphere.

Life on Earth

EARTH IS a unique place in the Solar System. It is the only planet to have significant liquid water on its surface; its surface is maintained at a liveable temperature by its breathable

Life on Earth is a delicate balance of many elements, and as we upset this balance, life becomes ever more unstable.

atmosphere; its rotational axis inclined enough to give seasons but not extremes of seasons like Uranus. The biosphere (the thin layer of land, air and water that supports all life) walks a knife-edge influenced by all these factors, and is increasingly being affected by human activities.

The oxygen content of the atmosphere is maintained by photosynthesis and, as humans destroy their vegetation, the balance between oxygen and carbon dioxide is upset. Emissions from the burning of fossil fuels have helped to increase the level of carbon dioxide. More carbon dioxide in the air increases the greenhouse effect, warming the surface further and melting the polar ice caps.

The ozone layer in the stratosphere, which lies above the troposphere, protects Earth's surface from harmful ultraviolet radiation emitted by the Sun. Man-made gases such as chlorofluorocarbons break down the ozone and so allow more harmful radiation through.

As more and more humans inhabit Earth, the fragile biosphere is being threatened. Mankind must learn to respect the factors that make Earth a living planet.

OUR PLACE IN THE UNIVERSE

IT IS almost certain that there is no other intelligent life in the Solar System. Astronomers are looking for intelligent life around other stars and extra-solar planets have been discovered. The Sun is just one of billions of stars within the Milky Way Galaxy, and the Galaxy is just one stellar system within the Universe so, statistically, life should exist elsewhere. But there are huge distances between stars and between galaxies, which makes it unlikely that we will ever detect life elsewhere.

The Moon

Our Nearest Neighbour

THE MOON is Earth's only natural satellite. Orbiting Earth from just over 350,000 to over 400,000 km (200,000 to 250,000 miles) away, it accompanies Earth around the Sun. The Moon is the only other body in the Solar System on which humans have stood.

The Moon is Earth's only natural satellite.

The Moon

Mean distance from Earth: 384,400 km (238,900 miles)

Synodic period (new moon to new moon): 29.530588 days

Orbital Period (Earth days): 27.3 days

Rotational period (Earth days): 27.3 days

Inclination of lunar equator to orbit: 5°09'

Inclination of lunar equator to ecliptic: 1°33'

Orbital eccentricity: 0.055

Diameter: 3,476 km (2,160 miles)

Mass: 7.349x1022 kg (1.620x1023 lbs) (0.0123 x Earth mass)

Average density relative to water: 3.34

Brightest magnitude (when full): -12.7

STRUCTURE AND COMPOSITION

ALTHOUGH SMALLER than the inner planets, the Moon can be classified as a terrestrial. It may have a solid, iron-rich core, less than 360 km (230 miles wide). Above this possible core lies the mantle, which comprises about 90 per cent of the lunar volume. The lack of any fluid core explains why the Moon has only a residual magnetic field, a field of about 1×10^{-7} of Earth's.

The crust varies in thickness from a few tens of kilometres beneath the maria (for explanation, see below) to more than

Mare Imbrium, the 'sea of rains', was so named because it was once believed the darker areas (maria) on the Moon were seas similar to Earth's.

100 km (230 miles) in the highlands. Under some of the basins, the crust has been weakened so much that the mantle has bulged outwards, fracturing the basin floors. At these points, the denser mantle material produces local fluctuations in the gravitational field; these regions of higher gravity are known as mascons (mass concentrations).

The Moon has a very tenuous atmosphere in which helium, neon, argon and radon have been detected. The virtual lack of atmosphere means hardly any erosion of surface features has taken place. It also offers little protection from the solar wind and micrometeorite impacts.

The lunar surface suffers extremes of temperature as it has so little atmosphere. It can fall to 93K (-180°C/-292°F) at night and rise to 403K (130°C/266°F). Radar scans by the Clementine spacecraft have revealed that within the 12 km- (7 mile-) deep South Pole-Aitken basin (the largest and deepest basin known in the Solar System) small amounts of water-ice may exist; sunlight has never penetrated into crater Shackleton which lies in the South Pole-Aitken basin.

The Aitken basin located in the lunar south polar region.

THE LUNAR SURFACE

JUST LOOKING at the Moon in the sky with the naked eye shows dark maria or 'seas' (singular *mare*) interspersed with lighter regions. It was once thought that the maria were liquid oceans, but telescopes revealed that they are areas of basaltic lava.

The most obvious features on the Moon are impact craters. These

Ptolemaeus is a very prominent walled plain in the central part of the near-side of the Moon.

range in size from tiny pits made by micrometeorites to the largest impact basins of well over a 1,000 km (600 miles) in diameter. The largest crater is Bailly with a diameter of 295 km (183 miles).

Ejecta thrown up by the impacts have created secondary impact craters. Some craters have ejecta blankets (layers of material thrown out at impact from a crater or basin) that stretch for hundreds of kilometres from the point of impact. The mountains and hills surrounding many craters were formed by huge lumps of ejecta flung out at the primary impact.

Rays emanating from some relatively young craters, like Tycho near the southern limb, are conspicuous signs of ejecta. The ejecta are brighter, rich in calcium and aluminium.

Most craters are circular, indicating that the impactor was vaporised and the resulting shock waves excavated the crater. Large craters often have central peaks, created when the central floor rebounded, and terraced walls that have collapsed.

VOLCANIC FEATURES

AS WELL as impact craters there are a few craters on the Moon that were caused by volcanism early in its history. The summit craters found on many domes are volcanic in origin, as are the rimless craters. Other signs of volcanism include the lunar domes – low swellings that resemble calderae – and sinuous rilles, which are collapsed lava tubes.

The most obvious sign of past volcanic activity are the maria. These were formed when large impacts created huge ringed basins, and subsequent volcanic outflows filled the flat floors with molten lava.

Collapsed lava tubes such as the Triesnecker Rille (pictured) are signs of previous volcanic activity on the Moon's surface.

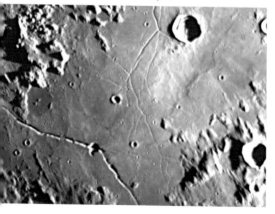

In addition to cratering and volcanism, the lunar crust has been deformed both vertically and horizontally. Wrinkle ridges were formed where the lunar crust contracted, while faults, scarps and rilles were produced as the crust stretched.

The far side of the Moon is riddled with numerous lunar craters.

THE FAR SIDE OF THE MOON

AS THE Moon is in synchronous rotation with Earth (it takes the same time to rotate on its axis as it does to orbit Earth) we always see the same hemisphere. The far side of the Moon, although never facing Earth, receives the same amount of sunlight as the near side.

When the far side was first photographed by the Soviet Luna 3 in 1959, it was discovered that it consisted of almost

Crater Daedalus, one of the features found on the far side of the Moon.

entirely lunar highlands with hardly any dark maria. Overall, about 16 per cent of the entire lunar surface is covered by maria; on the near side this rises to 31.2 per cent while only 2.6 per cent of the far side consists of these dark lava plains.

This is because the lunar crust is thicker on the far side so the lava did not get to the surface so easily. The difference in proportion of the lighter crust between the two hemispheres causes the Moon's centre of mass to be offset from its geometric centre by about 2 km (1.2 miles) towards Earth.

LUNAR ORIGIN

THE ORIGIN of the Moon is still in some doubt. Many astronomers believe a Mars-sized impact on Earth some 4,500,000,000 years ago threw enough material into Earth orbit to create the Moon. The denser material from the impacting body would have been pulled into Earth's core, leaving the Moon to form from the less dense, rocky material remaining in orbit.

This theory explains the relative lack of dense material at the lunar core, which cannot be explained easily if the Moon formed independently. The impact could have caused the tilt in the Earth's axis of rotation and explain why the orbit of the Moon is inclined by about 5 degrees to the ecliptic.

Other theories of lunar creation include the capture theory whereby the Moon formed independently of Earth and was subsequently pulled into Earth orbit, and the co-creation theory where the Moon formed independently alongside Earth.

Lunar craters Theophilus, Cyrillus and Catharina.

The Earth-Moon System

EARTH AND the Moon orbit their centre of mass, a point called the barycentre which is situated about 4,700 km (2,900 miles) from the centre of the Earth, well beneath Earth's surface.

Although Earth and the Moon are in synchronous rotation and we always see the same hemisphere, the effects of libration (irregularities in the lunar rotation) allow us to see 59 per cent of the lunar surface over a period of 30 years.

The Moon is gradually receding from Earth at a rate of about 3 cm per year. Earth's rotation is slowing by about 0.00001 of a second every century, enough for the Moon to be pulled forwards in its orbit, to speed up and thus move farther away. This keeps the total angular momentum of the system constant.

The Moon as seen from Apollo 11.

LUNAR PHASES

THE MOON orbits Earth every month. In this time, the geometry between the three bodies – Earth, the Moon and the Sun – changes.

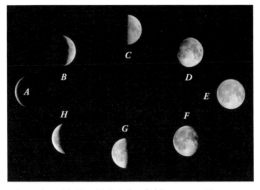

Lunar phases of the Moon (clockwise from far left): new moon (A), crescent moon (B, H), first quarter (C), gibbous moon (D, F), full moon (E), last quarter (G).

The Moon can only be seen where light from the Sun falls on its surface. At new moon, nothing of the Moon can be seen from Earth because it lies between Earth and the Sun with all the light falling on the hemisphere pointing away from Earth. At full moon, the Moon lies on the opposite side of Earth to the Sun so all the Sun's light falls on the hemisphere visible from Earth.

As the Moon continues in its orbit around Earth, different portions of the Moon's surface are illuminated as seen from Earth, giving the different phases. The best views of lunar features can be obtained near the terminator, the line between lunar night and day.

Tides on Earth are the result of the gravitational pull exerted by the Sun and the Moon.

TIDAL INFLUENCE

THE MOON exerts a gravitational pull on Earth. The clearest manifestation of this force is seen in Earth's ocean tides. On the side of Earth nearest to the Moon, the Moon has the greatest influence on the oceans, effectively pulling the water towards itself. This creates a bulge in the ocean.

On the opposite side of Earth, there is the least amount of pull from the Moon, so the water bulges in the opposite direction. The two bulges stay roughly aligned with the Earth-Moon line as Earth rotates, creating two tides each day.

The Moon is far smaller than the Sun but much closer to Earth and so has the greater gravitational effect on the oceans. When the Sun, Moon and Earth are aligned (at full and new moon), the tides are the greatest (the spring tides). When the Sun and Moon are at right angles to each other in the sky (at first and last quarter), the Sun's gravitational pull opposes that of the Moon's, giving the lesser 'neap' tides.

LUNAR ECLIPSES

SOMETIMES THE Moon passes into Earth's shadow. It does not happen every full moon because the Moon does not orbit in the same plane as the ecliptic. When it does, a lunar eclipse occurs.

The Moon at totality during a total lunar eclipse. It appears red because of sunlight reflected from Earth's atmosphere.

The Apollo Moon Landings

A TOTAL of 12 astronauts set foot on the Moon between 1969 and 1972. They visited six regions and brought back a total of 382 kg (842 lbs) of lunar material.

Exploring the nearest extraterrestrial body in space is an understandable goal. Before the Apollo programme, the lunar surface had been extensively studied by both Soviet and American spacecraft. A speech by President John F. Kennedy to Congress in 1961 promised to put a man on the Moon before 1970, and the space race began.

Buzz Aldrin (pictured) and Neil Armstrong were the first humans to set foot on the Moon.

This footprint on the Mare Tranquillitatis marks the Apollo 11 mission landing.

The first six Apollos were used to test the equipment including the huge Saturn V launch vehicles. Tragically, three astronauts were killed during ground tests in 1967, but success finally came when Neil Armstrong and Edwin 'Buzz' Aldrin stepped out into the Sea of Tranquillity in 1969.

Apollo 12 landed near the site of Surveyor 3, which had landed in the Oceanus Procellarum two years earlier. Parts of Surveyor were returned to Earth for analysis.

Apollo 14 landed in the Fra Mauro formation, part of the ejecta blanket associated with the Imbrium Basin. The astronauts of the last three Apollo missions covered far more ground than the early missions, with the help of lunar rovers.

Since the last man left the lunar surface in 1972, no plans have been made to return.

Apollo missions to the Moon

Apollo Mission	Landing date	Landing site
11	20 July 1969	Mare Tranquillitatis
12	19 November 1969	Oceanus Procellarum
14	31 January 1971	Fra Mauro
15	30 July 1971	Hadley-Apennine
16	21 April 1972	Descartes
17	11 December 1972	Taurus-Littrow

ASTEROIDS, COMETS AND METEORITES

Space Debris

T HE SUN and
planets formed
from a large,
contracting cloud of
dust and gas;
temperatures rose as
the Sun was born,
then gradually cooled
allowing different
elements to condense
out of the cloud.
Grains stuck together;
objects collided,
fragmented and
regrouped, forming planetesimals and planetary embryos, and
eventually the nine planets with their retinue of moons.

Even minute particles of debris can cause great damage to spacecraft in orbit due to the great speeds with which they are moving.

But not all of the material was swept up into planets. There
is still a great deal of debris left, ranging in size from grains of
dust to objects the size of Pluto.

Dust and debris pervade the whole of the Solar System, but
there are regions that have concentrations. The composition of
the debris varies with distance from the Sun. Of these, the region
nearest the Sun is the asteroid belt, where the majority of the

rocky asteroids lie. Beyond the orbit of Neptune is the Kuiper belt where rocky/icy bodies exist, and at the farthest edge of the Solar System is the Oort cloud – a reservoir of icy comets.

Not all debris is material left over from the Solar System's formation. Impacts still occur, and if they are on rocky bodies like the Moon or Mars, material can be flung out at such a velocity that it leaves its parent planet.

Other debris is man-made. Increasingly the space around Earth is becoming littered with dead satellites and parts of spacecraft.

Space debris can be dangerous if it falls to Earth, and even flecks of paint can cause damage to spacecraft in orbit because of the relative speeds involved.

Debris from defunct satellites and spacecraft in space can be dangerous if they fall to Earth.

Asteroids

SMALL, IRREGULARLY shaped, rocky bodies that lie predominantly in the inner solar system are called asteroids or minor planets. The largest known asteroid is Ceres with a

diameter of about 940 km (580 miles) but most asteroids (of which about 5,000 are known) are less than 100 km (60 miles) across.

Gaspra, one of the two asteroids seen close up by the planetary probe Galileo on its way to Jupiter.

THE ASTEROID BELT

A HIGH percentage of all asteroids orbit the Sun in the asteroid belt. These 'main belt' asteroids follow roughly circular orbits from 2 to 3.3 AU and have inclinations to the ecliptic of less than 20 degrees.

The total amount of mass in the asteroid belt is around 15 per cent of the Moon's mass. Asteroids are remnants of the solar nebula that failed to form a planet because of the gravitational tug between the Sun and Jupiter. Gaps have been created in the belt because of this tug-of-war. These Kirkwood gaps exist at distances where asteroids would orbit in a simple fraction of Jupiter's period (e.g. $\frac{1}{2}$, $\frac{1}{3}$, $\frac{2}{3}$ etc).

Asteroids vary in composition within the belt, depending on their distance from the Sun. Most are carbonaceous chondrites – primitive matter formed early in the age of the

Solar System. S-type asteroids have traces of metals and are found mainly in the inner part of the belt. M-type have a high metallic content. C-type are carbon-rich, very dark, and are found in the outer part of the belt.

The Hirayami families are groups of asteroids with the same orbital characteristics. More than 40 such families are known, some with more than 70 members. They are thought to be the remnants of shattered, larger objects.

Minor planets?: Asteroids Mathilde, Ida and Gaspra to scale.

Asteroid location

Type	Main position in Solar System
Aten	Within Earth's orbit
Apollo	Within Mars's orbit
Amor	Between Earth and Mars
Main belt	Between Mars and Jupiter
Trojan	At Jupiter's Lagrangian points
Centaur	Between Saturn and Neptune

OTHER GROUPS

WITHIN THE orbit of Mars lie the near-Earth objects (NEOs). Three different groups are classed as NEOs.

The Amors lie between Mars and Earth and do not cross Earth's orbit, but they can still approach Earth to within 0.3 AU (45,000,000 km or 28,000,000 miles).

The Apollos lie mainly beyond Earth, but their elliptical orbits cross Earth's on their approach to the Sun. The Atens lie mainly within Earth's orbit, but move out to aphelion (furthest point from the Sun) beyond Earth's orbit.

Within the orbit of planet Mars (pictured) lie three different groups of NEOs (near-Earth objects).

Earth is not the only planet to have close-passing asteroids. Some Apollo asteroids, including Icarus and Phaethon, cross the orbits of Venus and Mercury on their trips in towards the Sun.

Beyond the main belt are the Trojan asteroids. These lie at the Lagrangian points in Jupiter's orbit (where small bodies can maintain a stable orbit despite gravitational influences from the Sun and Jupiter). The Trojans are very dark bodies, and there may be many more than the 200 or so that have been discovered at present.

Centaurs are bodies in unstable orbits between Saturn and Neptune. The first Centaur, Chiron, was discovered in 1977 and classified as an asteroid, but during its perihelion it developed comet-like properties. The Centaurs are now believed to be part of the huge disc of rocky/icy objects known as the Kuiper belt.

Centaurs are bodies in unstable orbit between the planets Saturn (pictured) and Neptune.

THE ASTEROID-COMET CONNECTION

BEYOND NEPTUNE, at distances between 30 and 100 AU, is the Kuiper belt. It is estimated that 35,000 rocky/icy objects of around 100 to 200 km (60 to 120 miles) across and millions

An asteroid falls to Earth: Eros was once orbiting the Sun in the Asteroid belt.

of smaller bodies exist here, but because of their distance from Earth and their small size, only around 100 have so far been observed.

The Centaurs may be disturbed Kuiper belt objects, perturbed out of their original orbits into unstable, elliptical paths crossing the orbits of the gas giants – in a similar way that the Aten, Amor and Apollo asteroids may once have been part of the Asteroid belt.

Kuiper belt objects have a much higher ice content than bodies in the asteroid belt. Before the discovery of Chiron, asteroids and comets were

Interchangeable: Chiron (blue dot in this image) is classified as both an asteroid and a comet.

believed to be distinct classes of objects but, as Chiron approached the Sun in 1988, it produced a coma (a diffuse cloud of gas and dust that surrounds the nuclei of a comet as it approaches the Sun). It was then suggested that some asteroids could be the remnants of dead comets.

It now appears that there is no firm dividing line between asteroids and comets. Chiron is classified as both, being known as asteroid 2060 and comet Kowal-Meech-Belton.

Comets

COMETS CAN be the most spectacular objects in the Solar System with their tails stretching out across the night sky, although many more appear just as the faintest fuzzy patch in large telescopes.

Comets are not confined to the plane of the ecliptic and approach the Sun from every angle. Their orbits can be very elongated and they are categorised as either long- or short-period comets, according to the time it takes them to orbit the Sun, short period comets have orbital periods of less than 200 years.

Far away from the Sun, a comet resembles an asteroid: an inert, irregularly shaped, rocky body but, as these cometary nuclei lie far from the Sun in the Kuiper belt and the Oort cloud, they contain large amounts of ice. Comets are

The rocky-icy nucleus of Halley's comet as seen from the Giotto space probe.

Periodic comets get caught up by the gravity of major planets, such as Halley's comet, viewed here from Australia in March 1986.

composed of roughly 75 per cent ice and 25 per cent dust. They are sometimes described as 'dirty snowballs'; the dust resembles primitive carbonaceous chondritic material.

If comets are perturbed from their orbits, the gravitational field of the Sun may pull them in towards itself, and as they approach, they get gradually warmer.

At around the orbit of Jupiter (5 AU), the ices start to sublimate: changing from solid straight to gas. The gas forms the coma around the nucleus, a very tenuous atmosphere often pushed into a 'teardrop' shape by the solar wind. Comas can grow to be more than 100,000 km (60,000 miles) across. Beyond the visible coma is a large envelope of hydrogen that can extend out over millions of kilometres.

Observations of comet Hale-Bopp led to the discovery of a third type of cometary tail.

COMETARY TAILS

UNTIL 1997, it was believed that comets had two types of tail, the Type I ion (or gas) tail and the Type II dust tail.

As the ices sublimate, the ultraviolet radiation ionises the gases, knocking out electrons and creating positively charged ions. The ions stream out in the solar wind, always travelling directly away from the Sun, forming the straight ion tail. The magnetic fields within the ion tail of the comet cause the structure that is seen, and parts of the tail can sometimes become detached during what is known as a disconnection event.

The ion tail fluoresces (recaptured electrons emit light) and can be 1,000,000 km (600,000 miles) wide and 10,000,000 km (6,000,000 miles) long. Both the ion tail and the coma can be bluish in appearance because of the presence of carbon monoxide.

The pressure from the sunlight knocks the dust particles off the nucleus and out into space. The dust particles are left behind as the comet approaches its perihelion and form the curved dust tail, curved because of the path of the comet. Some dust tails are fan-shaped as different sized particles are pushed different distances from the nucleus.

Dust tails shine by reflected sunlight, producing a yellowish tinge, and are normally only one-tenth the length of the ion tail. Sometimes a comet is seen to have an 'antitail', a tail apparently pointing towards the Sun; this is the dust tail seen edge on.

A third type of tail was discovered in 1997 when observations of comet Hale-Bopp showed the existence of a sodium tail.

Comet Hale-Bopp was jointly discovered in 1995 by Alan Hale and Thomas Bopp.

NAMING COMETS

COMETS ARE usually named after the discoverer, or joint discoverers. Thus Hale-Bopp, the bright comet discovered in 1995, was named after Alan Hale and Thomas Bopp. Hale-Bopp delighted observers during 1997 by reaching a brilliant magnitude of 0.8 and showing distinct gas and dust tails.

Hale-Bopp is a long-period comet and has the designation 'C' followed by the year it was discovered, a letter indicating the fortnight in 1995 when it was found, and the number indicating the order of discovery during that fortnight: its full name is C/1995 O1 Hale-Bopp. Short-period comets are prefixed by the letter 'P' and a number that refers to the order of when the comet's orbit was established (Halley's comet is 1P/Halley).

The seventeenth-century astronomer, Edmund Halley, realised that Halley's comet had a 76-year orbital period.

Long-period comets are believed to originate primarily in the Oort cloud. Perturbations by close passages to planets (particularly Jupiter) can influence their orbits and deflect them into short-period orbits, but most short-period comets are believed to originate in the Kuiper belt.

COMET HALLEY

ONE OF the most famous comets is 1P/Halley. Named, not after its discoverer, but after Edmund Halley, who realised that the bright comet seen in 1531, 1607 and 1682 was the same object with a roughly 76-year orbital period. It is even featured on the Bayeaux Tapestry.

Detailed observations of Halley's comet were made during its last perihelion in 1986, including imaging its nucleus by sending the Giotto spacecraft directly into its coma. Halley's nucleus is about 16 x 8 x 8 km (10 x 5 x 5 miles), composed mainly of water-ice with a dark crust through which jets of gas and dust were seen to erupt.

Halley's comet is featured on the Bayeux Tapestry (c. 1077).

Meteorites

Up to 10 meteorites fall to Earth each day; this one was found in Leicestershire, UK, in December 1965.

EARTH IS constantly bombarded by interplanetary debris (meteoroids), much of which burns up in the atmosphere producing streaks of light known as meteors or shooting stars. Any fragments of material which survive the fall to Earth are known as meteorites.

Many thousands of meteorites fall to Earth each year, but only a fraction are seen to fall or are discovered on the ground. Many fall on remote and inhospitable land, or in the oceans.

Cosmic spherules – micrometeorites which become entirely molten – have been found in abundance in the ocean sediment. Cosmic dust that is even smaller (less than 0.01 mm/0.0004 in) is slowed down by the tenuous upper atmosphere and does not melt at all.

Larger bodies form a glassy fusion crust: they can lose up to 50 per cent of their mass as they melt. The atmospheric gases around a larger body become ionised, causing a bright streak of light. A brighter streak is termed a fire-ball, and if the body explodes, it is called a bolide.

METEORITE COMPOSITION

THE ANALYSIS of recovered samples suggests that most meteorites are fragments of asteroids, with a few being impact ejecta from the Moon or Mars. There are three main types of meteorite: stony, stony-iron and iron.

Stony meteorites consist mostly of silicate minerals with a small proportion of nickel and iron. There are two main types: chondrites and achondrites. The majority are chondrites – iron and magnesium-bearing silicates containing chondrules. Chondrules are small, spherical, solidified droplets, formed during lightning discharges in the solar nebula or during an impact. Achondrites have no chondrules, contain very little iron and nickel and resemble volcanic material.

This six-pound meteorite was found in a pasture in 1994, the first to be recovered in Canada since 1972.

Iron meteorites contain an average of 90 per cent iron and nickel. They are subdivided according to the percentage of nickel: the hexahedrites with less than six per cent, octahedrites with more than six per cent and the nickel-rich ataxites.

Stony-iron meteorites are a relatively small group containing about 50 per cent nickel and iron and 50 per cent silicates.

Some asteroids consist of primitive material: material that has not been significantly altered since the formation of the Solar System 4,600,000,000 years ago. The carbonaceous chondrite meteorites are the most primitive and are examples of the material from which the Solar System formed.

Larger asteroids have some degree of differentiation where the heavier elements have sunk to the middle, leaving a rocky (silicate) crust. Stony meteorites are fragments of this crust, while iron meteorites come from the core. Achondrites are believed to be mainly from planetary surfaces.

In a meteor shower, all meteors seem to come from one direction.

METEORS

COMETS LOSE a lot of dust as they approach the Sun and if Earth travels through the path of a comet, the dust is burned up, producing meteor showers. The meteors appear to come from a single point (the radiant) and are named after the constellation in which the radiant appears.

Space debris which does not burn up may land on Earth as a meteorite.

Selected Meteor Showers: Essential Data

Shower	Parent Comet	Activity Dates
Quadrantids*	–	1–6 January
Lyrids	Thatcher	19–25 April
Eta Aquarids	Halley	24 April–20 May
Perseids	Swift-Tuttle	25 July–20 August
Orionids	Halley	15 October–2 November
Leonids	Tempel-Tuttle	15–20 November
Geminids	Phaethon (asteroid)	7–15 December

(*Quadrans is an ancient constellation)

THE SUN

Our Star

THE SUN is a star. It shines because it creates its own energy in its core. The Sun is very important for life on Earth: all heat, light and energy come from the Sun.

A STAR IS BORN

STARS FORM from cold, dense clouds in the interstellar medium: the huge clouds of dust and gas that lie between the stars.

The interstellar medium is composed mainly of hydrogen and helium, but when past generations of stars died, they shed

The Sun: all heat, light and energy on Earth comes from it.

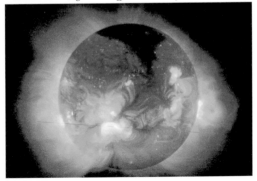

The Sun: Essential Data

Mean distance from Earth: 149,600,000 km (93,000,000 miles)

Light travel time to Earth: 8.3 min

Mean angular diameter: 32 arc min

Diameter: 1,392,000 km (865,000 miles)

Mass: 1.9891×10^{30} kg (4.3852×10^{30} lbs) (332,950 Earth mass)

Mean photospheric temperature: 5,800 K (5,527°C/9,980°F)

Mean internal temperature: 15,000,000 K
    (15,000,000°C/27,000,000°F)

Luminosity (the Sun's energy radiated per second):
3.83×10^{26} watts

Spectral type*: G2

Apparent magnitude: -26.8

(*See page 131 for definition of spectral type)

the heavier elements (elements heavier than hydrogen and helium) made during their life back into the interstellar medium. Thus younger stars, like the Sun, contain these heavy elements. The Sun's mass is made up of 71 per cent hydrogen, 27 per cent helium and 1–2 per cent other elements.

Sometimes a trigger is necessary to start a cloud contracting. This could be the gravitational tug of a passing star, the density wave within the arm of a spiral galaxy or the shock wave from an exploding supernova. Some astronomers believe a nearby supernova started the cloud contracting from which the Sun formed, 4,600,000,000 years ago.

As the cloud contracted, the pressure and temperature rose at the centre until it was so hot and the pressures so great that nuclear fusion began. Nuclear fusion is the power within all stars, and in the Sun vast amounts of hydrogen are being

Dust clouds such as the Trifid Nebula (pictured) are the birthplace of stars.

changed into helium, producing energy. A star is said to be born when nuclear fusion starts.

All through a star's life there is a balancing act between gravity (trying to make the star contract) and pressures from within trying to push the star apart. A star is most stable when it is burning the hydrogen in its core. At this stage it is called a main sequence star, and it will spend most of its life on the main sequence. The Sun is currently at this stage of its life and will continue to burn its core hydrogen for another 5,000,000,000 or 6,000,000,000 years.

OLD AGE AND DEATH

WHEN ALL the hydrogen fuel in the core has been used up, the Sun will start to burn the hydrogen in its atmosphere in a series of shells. As the source of energy moves outwards, the Sun will expand and cool, becoming a red giant.

Once all the hydrogen has been used up, the Sun will collapse. The core will heat up again until it is hot enough for nuclear fusion to start once more, this time burning the helium and producing carbon.

Helium burning lasts for a much shorter time than hydrogen burning and eventually all the core helium will be used up. Helium shell burning then starts, but when the Sun collapses this time, the core will not heat up enough for any further nuclear fusion to occur. The Sun will become a white dwarf, gradually cooling and fading.

This planetary nebula, the NGC 2440, is an ageing star.

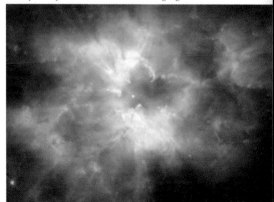

Solar Structure

THE CORE of the Sun is a region about 20 per cent of the solar diameter. Through the core and a region extending more than 70 per cent of the Sun's radius, energy is radiated outwards. Above this lies the convection zone, about 30 per cent of a solar radius deep where the principal method of energy movement is convection: the hot material rises to the top where it cools and sinks back down.

The radiation produced in the core is in the form of gamma rays: the most energetic radiation. Radiation can be thought of as consisting of photons, 'packets' of energy. The type of radiation depends on how much energy these photons have. As the photons move outwards, they lose energy, and so become x-rays, then ultraviolet, visible and infrared. It can take a photon hundreds of thousands of years to reach the photosphere because it continually gets scattered, absorbed and re-emitted during its journey.

We see the Sun in the sky as a well-defined disc of very bright light (*never* look directly at the Sun as permanent eye damage can result). This is because our eyes have evolved to respond to the radiation we call visible light. The Sun emits across the whole of the electromagnetic spectrum, but the majority of visible light is produced within a 500 km- (300 mile-) deep region – a very thin region compared to the solar diameter. This is the photosphere – sometimes called the surface.

Beyond the photosphere is the chromosphere – 2,000 to 10,000 km (1,200 to 6,200 miles) thick – and beyond that lies the outer atmosphere, the corona, which extends out for many thousands of kilometres and merges with the interplanetary medium. Temperature increases across the chromosphere to reach around 10,000K (10,000°C/18,000°F) at the bottom of a transition zone. Through this zone, the temperature soars to around 1,000,000K (1,000,000°C/1,800,000°F). It is not fully understood why the corona should be heated to such an amount, but magnetic reconnection events (when magnetic fields lines reconnect after temporary separation) could be the cause – explosive energy is produced when magnetic field lines recombine.

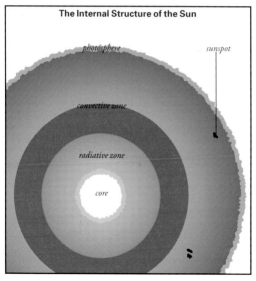

The Internal Structure of the Sun

photosphere

sunspot

convective zone

radiative zone

core

SOLAR NEUTRINOS

AS WELL as producing photons, nuclear fusion creates neutrinos. Neutrinos are elementary particles with negligible or no mass, and no charge. They do not interact much with ordinary matter, and instead of taking hundreds of thousands of years to leave the Sun, like photons, they pass through almost instantaneously and are emitted at the rate of about 6×10^{14} neutrinos every square metre of the Sun's surface per second.

They also pass rapidly through Earth. Neutrino detectors have been built, deep underground, but results show only a third of the expected total of the neutrinos. Reasons for this have been devised, but no theory has yet been generally accepted.

SUNSPOTS

WHEN OBSERVING the Sun in white light, dark spots can sometimes be seen on the solar disc. These sunspots have been observed regularly since the early nineteenth century, and are good indicators of the Sun's activity: a lot of spots indicates an active Sun.

Sunspot activity fluctuates over a period of roughly 11 years which is commonly called the solar cycle. In fact, because of magnetic effects, it is actually a cycle of about 22 years, which is called the magnetic solar cycle.

The Sun has an overall magnetic field similar in strength to Earth's. However the Sun consists of a plasma – the hydrogen is at such a high temperature (from about 15,000,000K (15,000,000°C /27,000,000°F) at the centre to about 6,000K (5,727°C /10,340° F) at the photosphere) that the electrons are stripped off the hydrogen atoms leaving a sea of positively charged ions and negatively charged electrons. Within such a plasma, magnetic field lines become trapped – they cannot

The Sudbury Neutrino Observatory, in Ontario, Canda.

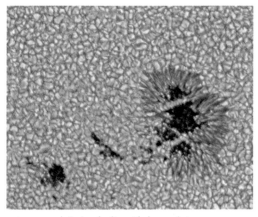

A sunspot on the Sun's surface lies amid solar granulation.

move freely through the charged particles, so as the Sun rotates and as the plasma moves as a result of convection, the magnetic field lines get tangled up and packed together in localised regions.

Heat to these regions is constricted and they appear dark (cooler) against the surrounding photosphere. In the dark umbra of sunspots, temperatures can be 1,000K (1,000°C/1,800°F) lower than the photosphere; the lighter penumbral regions have temperatures around 5,500K (5,227°C/9,440°F). Magnetic fields within sunspots can be up to 10,000 times the usual strength of the Sun's field.

EXPLOSIVE EVENTS

OBSERVING THE Sun in other types of radiation, like X-rays, reveals a dynamic and turbulent body. A continuous stream of particles, mainly protons and electrons, is emitted from the Sun. This is the solar wind. Solar flares eject huge amounts of plasma and energy into the solar wind, while coronal mass ejections (CMEs) are enormous bubbles of plasma that expand through the corona and out into space.

Gusts in the solar wind from flares and CMEs can cause magnetic storms, interrupt communications and create power surges on Earth.

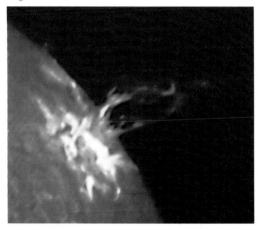

A solar prominence erupts from the Sun.

Solar Eclipses

THE MOON and the Sun appear roughly the same size in the sky. The Moon is actually about 400 times smaller than the Sun, but also 400 times nearer. During a total solar eclipse, the Moon covers the photosphere of the Sun, revealing the chromosphere and the ghostly corona.

The solar corona at total eclipse.

If the Moon travelled round Earth in the same plane that Earth orbits the Sun (the ecliptic), then a solar eclipse would happen every new moon. However, the Moon's orbit is inclined by about 5 degrees to the ecliptic, so sometimes the Moon passes above or below the Sun in the sky. Only when the Moon is in Earth's orbital plane at new moon will a solar eclipse occur.

The orbits of the Moon and Earth are not circular, so the angular diameters of the Moon and Sun seen in the sky vary. Thus sometimes the Moon appears smaller than the Sun and an annular eclipse occurs; a ring of the photosphere still surrounds the Moon and the corona is not seen.

Observers will only see a total solar eclipse if they are in the umbral shadow (main shadow) of the Moon. In the penumbral shadow (partial shadow) a partial eclipse of the Sun is observed.

As the final sliver of Sun disappears during a total eclipse, the last of the photospheric light shines through the valleys on the lunar limb: an effect called Baily's Beads. The beads of light wink out until sometimes only one is left: the diamond ring.

When the last of the photospheric light disappears, the ethereal corona comes into view. The shape of the corona varies: at solar maximum it is concentrated around the solar equator, at solar minimum it shines right round the Sun.

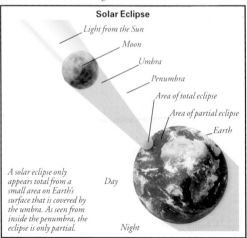

Solar Eclipse

Light from the Sun

Moon

Umbra

Penumbra

Area of total eclipse

Area of partial eclipse

Earth

A solar eclipse only appears total from a small area on Earth's surface that is covered by the umbra. As seen from inside the penumbra, the eclipse is only partial.

Day

Night

THE STARS

Introduction

AWAY FROM street lights, it is possible to see more than 2,000 stars with the naked eye.

The Sun is our nearest star, which is why it appears so large in our skies. In fact, it is quite a small star. The next nearest star, Proxima Centauri, lies more than four light years away: it would take over four years to get there, travelling at the speed of light.

Most other stars appear only as points of light because of the huge distances involved; only recently have powerful telescopes

The constellation of Gemini (pictured) is highest in the sky from January to February as seen from the northern hemisphere.

The double cluster of stars in the constellation of Perseus.

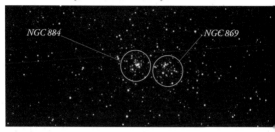

NGC 884

NGC 869

been able to resolve another star's disc – and this was of Betelgeuse, a large red supergiant lying relatively close to Earth.

From ancient times, patterns have been superimposed on the stars. Stars do move with respect to each other, but because they lie at such vast distances from us, this movement is hardly noticeable over a human life-span. Thus the ancient patterns are still recognisable today. The star with the highest proper motion (movement across the sky) is Barnard's star which moves 10.3 arc seconds per year.

The whole starry sky does move – rising in the east and setting in the west. This apparent movement results from Earth rotating on its axis. The stars rise about four minutes earlier each night because Earth is also moving along the path of its orbit. As Earth orbits the Sun, different parts of the night sky become visible over the year.

Some stars remain visible all year round. These are the circumpolar stars that lie near the poles. Polaris marks the north celestial pole, and is called the Pole Star, but no bright star marks the south celestial pole.

The constellations of Orion, Canis Major and Canis Minor.

The Constellations

THE SKY is split into 88 constellations. Most of the constellations in the northern hemisphere are named after Greek and Roman myths, while those in the southern hemisphere include more modern objects. The southern sky was not mapped until the nineteenth century.

Very few of the constellations resemble the object after which they are named. Orion, the hunter, for example, does have a shape that could be a tunic, with a recognisable belt and sword. But although it appears that the stars within the belt lie

The constellation of Capricornus.

close to each other, it is just a line-of-sight effect. In reality, stars within constellations are generally totally unconnected.

Just looking at the sky shows a difference in brightness between stars, some of which show faint colouring – an indication of temperature. Astronomers use magnitudes to indicate a star's brightness, the brighter the star the smaller the magnitude: the brightest star is Sirius at magnitude -1.46 while the faintest naked-eye stars are about +6.

This apparent magnitude is how the stars appear in the sky and takes no account of their distance. Absolute magnitude is calculated as if all stars were at the same distance from Earth and gives a measure of their luminosity (energy output).

Starlight

DESPITE THE huge distances, it is possible to glean information about the stars from their spectra. If a prism is placed in the Sun's light, the colours of the rainbow are produced. The white light of the Sun is a combination of the colours seen in the rainbow. The prism splits white light into the visible spectrum according to its energy, or wavelength.

The visible spectrum is just a small part of the electromagnetic spectrum. Light is radiation, and radiation varies from the high energy (small wavelength) gamma rays down to the low energy (long wavelength) radio waves.

Using a spectroscope, the light from stars can also be spread out in a spectrum. Bands of bright and dark can be seen in stellar spectra. These bands (spectral lines) represent different elements – radiation of different, distinct, wavelengths is emitted when electrons are dislodged and absorbed by different gases at high temperature, as in a star's atmosphere. Thus the chemical composition of stars can be determined.

Stars are classified according to their spectra. The main classes are O, B, A, F, G, K and M. O types are the hottest, M the coolest. Each class is further divided. The Sun is a G2 star.

Spectral lines are often displaced from where they should be. This is a result of the star's motion. If a star is moving away, the radiation is redshifted – 'stretched out' towards the red part of the spectrum.

Many stars belong to binary or multiple systems. Their interactions can give us even more information. Visual binaries are systems where both stars can be observed. Plotting their movement over time gives the orbital period, which together with their separation, can reveal their masses. Spectroscopic binaries are systems where the stars are not resolved (cannot be seen separately), but changes within the spectrum reveal their movements.

Astrometric binaries are systems where only one star is observed, but this star is seen to 'wobble' as it moves through the sky. The wobble is due to the gravitational tug of an unseen companion. In 1844, the brightest star in the sky, Sirius, was discovered to be an astrometric binary. Its white dwarf companion, Sirius B, was first observed in 1862.

The colours of light in a rainbow represent just a small part of the electromagnetic spectrum.

THE HERTZSPRUNG-RUSSELL DIAGRAM

DURING ITS LIFE, the Sun will emit different amounts of radiation, its temperature will change and its size will fluctuate. All of these changes can be represented on a Hertzsprung-Russell (H-R) diagram. Named after Danish astronomer Einjar Hertzsprung (1873–1967) and American astronomer Henry Norris Russell (1877–1957), it is one of the most informative diagrams in astronomy. The H-R diagram gives a lot of information about stars just by plotting their luminosity (brightness) against surface temperature. The temperature axis at the bottom runs backwards from hot to cool. It can be looked at as a snapshot of the Milky Way Galaxy as it is seen today.

The majority of stars, like the Sun, lie on a wavy band that includes dim, cool stars in the bottom right-hand corner through to hot, bright stars at top left. These 'main sequence' stars are relatively stable and are burning their core hydrogen.

A group of stars lying in the right-hand corner of the H-R diagram are cool, but fairly luminous stars. They appear luminous because they are so big. They are the red giants and supergiants – stars that have finished their core burning and are burning the elements in their envelopes.

To the bottom left are another groups of stars: the white dwarfs. These are stars that have finished burning their nuclear fuel. They have collapsed, and will gradually cool and fade.

The colours on this diagram are a visual representation of the heat of the stars: blue on the left being the coolest; to red on the right being the hottest.

The Hertzsprung-Russell Diagram came about after Hertzsprung and Russell, who each had separately produced similar diagrams, realised how important such a diagram could be in understanding more about the stars in our galaxy.

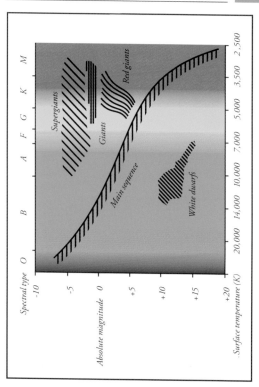

Stellar Evolution

IF A COLD cloud of molecular hydrogen lying in the interstellar medium collapses, the temperature at its centre can rise until it is hot enough for nuclear fusion to start. At this point a star is born.

Protostars lie to the right of the main sequence on the H-R diagram. They are luminous because they are large and they move to the left on the diagram as they contract and heat up.

The Cat's Eye Nebula is a dramatic planetary nebula.

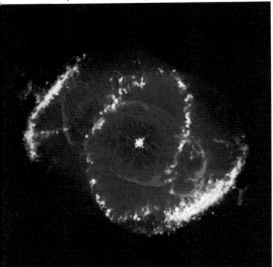

Eventually hydrogen burning starts and the star becomes a member of the main sequence.

Stars spend the greatest proportion of their lives on the main sequence, but the more massive the star, the shorter this time is. More massive stars have higher core temperatures and thus burn their fuel more quickly. When a star has finished burning the hydrogen in its core, it burns the hydrogen in its atmosphere in a series of shells. The star expands and its surface temperature falls. The star becomes a red giant (or supergiant depending on its original mass) and evolves to the right of the main sequence on the H-R diagram.

While hydrogen shell burning occurs, helium builds up in the star's core which contracts and heats up. Eventually the temperature is high enough for helium fusion to start. In stars of around the Sun's mass, this helium burning starts rapidly in a helium flash.

For a brief time, the star burns its helium in the core, producing carbon and oxygen, and when the core helium is depleted, helium shell burning occurs. The more massive the star, the more times it goes through this process, producing different elements. The heaviest element which can be produced inside stars is iron; anything heavier is produced in a supernova explosion.

While stars expand and contract using up all their fuel, they pass back and forth on the H-R diagram to the right of the main sequence. This area is known as the instability strip. It is during this stage that some of the outer atmospheres of stars are puffed off to produce the weird and wonderful planetary nebulae. Although nothing to do with planets, they received this misnomer when early observers saw planet-like discs through their telescopes.

STELLAR DEATH

ONCE ALL the fuel has been finished, the remnant of a star collapses. For remnants less than 1.4 solar masses (the Chandrasekhar limit), the force between electrons stops the collapse. The star has now become a white dwarf.

Remnants of the star over the Chandrasekhar limit collapse further until the force between neutrons halts the contraction. It is now a neutron star. Rotating neutron stars emit radiation in a narrow beam, and if the beam is directed towards Earth, we observe a pulsar. Some neutron stars rotate in times as short as 0.0016 seconds.

If a stellar remnant is more than two or three solar masses, it continues to collapse. The object becomes so small and dense that its gravitational field is strong enough to stop anything being emitted; it becomes a black hole.

Shells of gas emanating from an old, collapsing star.

A white dwarf (pictured at the centre of a nebula) is a small, dense star with only 1 per cent of the Sun's diameter.

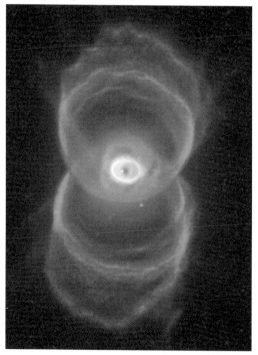

Variable Stars

STARS THAT vary because of some internal factor are intrinsic variables; others, like binary stars, are extrinsic.

PULSATING STARS

SOME STARS vary in brightness because they pulsate; they expand and contract significantly, some in a periodic way.

Semiregular variables are giant and supergiant stars, like Betelgeuse in Orion which varies in magnitude from about 0.3 to 0.9 in 5.8 years.

The variable star, Mira, varies in brightness over time.

Mira at low brightness

Mira at high brightness

Long-period Mira variables (named after the star Mira in the constellation Cetus) are cool red giants. The diameter of Mira changes by about 20 per cent over a period of 330 days, and its surface temperature varies from 1,900K to 2,600K (1,627°C/2,327°F to 2,960°C/4,220°F), making it alter from below naked-eye visibility to magnitude 1.7.

A Hubble Space Telescope image of Betelgeuse, a supergiant star in the constellation of Orion.

Cepheid variables, named after delta Cephei in Cepheus, are yellowish giants and supergiants. They vary in brightness in well-defined periods which are directly related to their luminosity. Type I Cepheids (young population I stars) are about four times more luminous than Type II, also known as W Virginis stars which are less massive, population II (older) stars.

Type I Cepheids vary over periods from about one to 10 days, while Type II vary over longer periods up to 80 days. These periods are very useful in determining their brightness and thus their distances and Cepheids are often used as distance indicators.

RR Lyrae stars (named after the star RR in Lyra) are old giants often found in globular clusters, which vary over periods of less than a day.

ERUPTIVE STARS

FLARE STARS including UV Ceti variables (named after the star UV in Cetus) are cool, low-luminosity, main sequence stars that undergo frequent outbursts. They can brighten by a few magnitudes in timescales of a few seconds. The flares are thought to be similar to solar flares, but because the stars are of low magnitude, a greater effect is seen.

BINARY STARS

THE SUN is unusual in being a star on its own. Many stars are members of binary or multiple systems that are bound gravitationally. Some stars are so close to each other that material flows between them and this has a profound effect on their evolution.

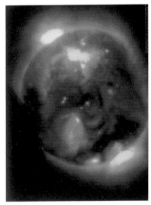

If a binary system is seen edge-on, eclipses between the two stars can occur, giving variations in brightness. Analysis of the light curve (the fluctuation in brightness over time) can reveal information about the size and luminosity of the pair. Algol, in Perseus, is an eclipsing binary.

The Sun (seen here through X-rays) is unusual in being a star on its own.

The constellation of Taurus includes the 'T' star after which the young, unstable Tauri stars are named. If all star points within the constellation are joined up, they form the outline of a bull.

Cataclysmic variables are binaries that are so close, material is pulled from one component to the other, sometimes causing an eruption and a consequential brightening in magnitude. One component is often a white dwarf. Novae (from the Latin meaning 'new') are cataclysmic variables which can brighten by 10 magnitudes or more.

OTHER VARIABLES

AS YOUNG stars evolve on to the main sequence, they are very unstable and thus can vary in brightness. T Tauri stars (named after the star T in Taurus) are examples of such very young stars.

R Coronae Borealis stars (named after the star R in Corona Borealis) are stars that dim periodically. They are cool, carbon-rich supergiants and their dramatic drops in brightness, by as much as a factor of 10,000, are thought to be caused by clouds of sooty dust ejected from their atmospheres.

GALAXIES

Discovering Galaxies

THE SOLAR System lies in the Milky Way Galaxy, a system containing around 100 billion stars. Throughout the Universe lie billions of other galaxies, many much larger than the Milky Way, but it was only in 1923 that observations confirmed these other stellar systems lie beyond the Milky Way.

THE MESSIER CATALOGUE

CHARLES MESSIER (1730–1817) was a French astronomer with an interest in comets. He discovered about 15 comets in his lifetime, but he is principally remembered for the catalogue of non-comets he compiled in 1781.

When comets approach the Sun, they are first seen as hazy patches of nebulosity. During Messier's search for these objects, he became aware of some patches that looked like comets, but which remained in the same position night after night. In order not to keep mistaking them as comets, he compiled a list of around 100 objects. Objects in the Messier catalogue are known by their Messier number: their number in the catalogue prefixed by the letter 'M'.

These objects fascinated other astronomers, including William Herschel (1738–1822) and his son, John (1792–1871), who continued to list the positions of comet-like objects. Subsequently J.L.E. Dreyer (1852–1926) published the New General Catalogue, and objects are also known by their NGC numbers.

The Andromeda galaxy (M31) lies within the Andromeda constellation.

In 1845, Lord Rosse (1800–67) used his mammoth telescope with a mirror 2 m (6 ft) across to view M51 (NGC5194), and discovered that it had a spiral structure. A great debate followed: were these patches of nebulosity far away stellar systems or were they smaller objects closer to home?

The debate was ended when the American astronomer, Edwin Hubble (1889–1953), observed Cepheid variables within M31 (NGC224). Using the known period-luminosity law for Cepheids, Hubble worked out that M31 lay 900,000 light years away. In fact it is now known to lie 2,250,000 light years away, but Hubble's result had showed that other stellar systems (galaxies) existed: the Milky Way was not the whole Universe.

A scale model (1:24) of Lord Rosse's gigantic telescope, erected at Birr in Ireland in 1845.

Nebulae

NOT ALL the patches of nebulosity in the Messier catalogue are other galaxies. Within the Milky Way lie vast amounts of dust and gas from which stars are born. When the protostars heat the clouds, the dust and gas glow, showing up in small telescopes as hazy patches.

The faint red tinge in Orion's sword, visible even with the naked eye under good sky conditions, is one such nebula. The Orion Nebula, M42 (NGC1976), is an emission nebula. Young stars (four of which, the Trapezium, can be seen in some photographs) heat the surrounding gas and dust until it ionises – electrons are stripped off the (predominantly) hydrogen

The bright Orion Nebula (M42) is one of the Galaxy's sites of new star formation.

atoms. Emission nebulae appear red because recombining hydrogen atoms emit principally red light.

Dark nebulae, like the beautiful Horsehead Nebula (NGC2024) near Orion's belt, are clouds of dust and gas with no nearby stars to heat them. The Horsehead is visible because it is silhouetted against an emission nebula.

The Crab Nebula (M1): the stellar remains of a supernova last seen from Earth in 1054.

The Beehive Cluster is an example of an open cluster.

Reflection nebulae glow because light from nearby stars reflects off dust grains. The nebulae appear blue because the dust grains scatter the blue light more than red, just like in Earth's sky. A reflection nebula lies amongst the Pleiades, M45 (NGC1432).

Other objects within Messier's catalogue are stars at various stages of their life. The very first object, M1 (NGC1952), the Crab Nebula, is in fact a supernova remnant. In 1054, a massive star blew up as a supernova, scattering its material. The material is ionised by ultraviolet radiation emitted by the pulsar at the core of the supernova.

Other stars that have evolved off the main sequence and have lost part of their outer atmosphere are the planetary nebulae. The Ring Nebula, M57 (NGC6720), in Lyra is one visible through small telescopes. The Hubble Space Telescope has photographed many more of these rather beautiful objects.

Clusters of stars also appear in the Messier Catalogue. Through limited magnification, such clusters appear as amorphous blobs. M44 (NGC2632), Praesepe or the Beehive Cluster, is an example of an open or galactic cluster. Associations of stars form from the same collapsing cloud and when young, can still be observed fairly close together.

Globular clusters like M92 (NGC6341) in Hercules, are spherical groups of old stars.

The Milky Way

OUR GALAXY, the Milky Way, is named after the faint band of light that can be seen (from dark sites) crossing the night sky. This band is light from thousands of stars lying in the plane of the galaxy.

The Milky Way is a faint band of light produced by thousands of distant stars.

The Milky Way is a spiral galaxy; shaped like two fried eggs laid back-to-back; the plane is the egg whites, and the central nucleus forms the yolks. The Sun lies about two-thirds of the way out from the centre within the Orion spiral arm.

If you could travel out from the Milky Way and look down upon the plane, spiral arms would be seen. These spiral patterns are caused by density waves sweeping through the dust and gas lying in the plane, compressing the clouds and starting star formation. Young stars shine more brightly than older stars, so the young starlight briefly picks out the spiral pattern. As the stars age and dim, the density wave moves on, creating another spiral of new stars.

Most of the objects in the Messier Catalogue that are not other galaxies lie in the plane of the Milky Way. As most of the dust and gas lies here, it is where the majority of star formation occurs. The exception is the globular clusters. These surround the galactic nucleus in the Galactic Halo, and it was their distribution in the sky that led astronomers to pinpoint the Galactic Centre.

Globulars consist of old, population II stars that formed billions of years ago when the galaxy itself was forming.

THE GALACTIC CENTRE

AT THE heart of the Milky Way lies a black hole candidate. There are two types of black hole: the endpoints of massive stars, and the super-massive black holes that are believed to lie at the centre of most galaxies.

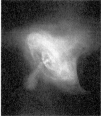

The centre of the galaxy lies in the direction of the constellation Sagittarius (Sgr). Within this constellation is a strong radio source, Sgr A which contains a compact source, Sgr A*. Sgr A* appears to be an object of 2,500,000 solar masses, contained within an area less than one light year across. Astronomers suggest that it is a black hole with matter spiralling into it via an accretion disc.

It is believed that a black hole (pictured) lies at the heart of the Milky Way Galaxy.

Galaxy Types

EDWIN HUBBLE continued studying galaxies, and he drew up a 'tuning fork' classification scheme which is still used today. Broadly, galaxies can be split into three main types: spiral, elliptical and irregular. The tuning fork diagram deals with the ellipticals and spirals.

The tuning fork diagram, as originally devised by Edwin Hubble, is used to classify galaxy types.

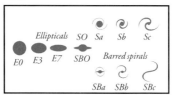

ELLIPTICALS

THE MAJORITY of galaxies are elliptical. This class contains both the largest and smallest of galaxies. They are classified according to how they appear in the sky, no correction being made for the angle from which we view them. There are eight sub-categories, E0 to E7, the number indicating how elliptical they appear. An E0 appears circular, and E7 is the most eccentric.

SPIRALS

SPIRALS ARE sub-classified into ordinary spirals (S) and barred spirals (SB), where the spiral arms start from a 'bar' instead of directly from the nucleus. They are further subdivided into a, b and c: Sa and SBa galaxies have large nuclei

A spiral galaxy (M51).

and tightly wound arms; Sc and SBc have small nuclei and loosely wound arms. A galaxy lying between classes a and b, for example, would be designated Sab. The Milky Way is either an Sbc or SBbc; recent observations suggest that its nucleus is elongated into a bar. Flocculent spirals have clumpy, chaotic and ill-defined arms. Spirals with 'copy book' shapes are termed grand design spirals and have thin, long arms.

LENTICULAR

BETWEEN THE two classes of ellipticals and spirals lie the lenticular or lens-shaped galaxies. Designated S0 or SB0, they have a nucleus surrounded by a disc, but no spiral structure.

IRREGULARS

GALAXIES THAT cannot be included in the main classification are termed irregulars. Many galaxies have suffered gravitational interactions, some being completely pulled apart like the two Magellanic clouds, which are small, irregular galaxies visible from the southern hemisphere that have been disrupted by the gravitational field of the Milky Way. Others are merging, like the Antennae Galaxy, and some have completely merged, like the Cartwheel Galaxy.

Galaxy Evolution

THE HUBBLE Classification scheme was once believed to be evolutional: either elliptical galaxies evolved into spirals, or vice versa. This is not now thought to be the case, although there is still no agreed theory on galaxy formation.

Galaxy formation is believed to have started 300,000 years after the Big Bang, when slight fluctuations in the primordial gas that pervaded the whole Universe began to grow into

protogalaxies. There are two main rival theories: the 'top-down' and 'bottom-up'.

In the top-down theory, the gas collapses into large, flattened clouds that fragment into individual galaxies. Ellipticals would have formed in the densest parts where star formation would have proceeded rapidly before the protogalaxy collapsed further, thus explaining their composition of predominantly older,

Elliptical galaxies can be dwarfs or giants.

Interacting galaxies NGC 2207 and IC 2163.

population II stars. Spirals would have formed in the less dense regions, the cloud collapsing into a flattened, rotating disc with star formation occurring first in the original spheroidal shape (explaining the halo of older stars) and later in the disc (explaining the predominantly younger, population I stars in the discs of spirals).

In the bottom-up theory, the primordial fluctuations would have created individual protogalaxies which would have then clustered together, some merging to form the larger galaxies. Spiral galaxies would have formed by slower accumulation of fragments than the giant ellipticals.

Large-Scale Structure

GALAXIES ARE not spread evenly throughout the Universe. Many are gravitationally bound in small groups and clusters, the clusters themselves forming giant superclusters. On the scale of superclusters, galaxies are confined to filaments with large voids between, rather like the soap film on bubbles.

THE LOCAL GROUP

THE MILKY WAY belongs to the Local Group, a cluster with around 30 known members within about 6,000,000 light years. The largest member is the Andromeda Galaxy, a spiral galaxy,

half as massive again as the Milky Way.

The Milky Way is the next massive member, followed by the spiral Triangulum Galaxy and the irregular Large and Small Magellanic Clouds. Most of the other members are dwarf ellipticals.

Our galaxy, the Milky Way, belongs to the Local Group, a relatively small cluster of galaxies.

CLUSTERS AND SUPERCLUSTERS

THE NEAREST rich cluster to the Local Group is the Virgo Cluster, containing more than 1,000 galaxies. The cluster is dominated by three giant ellipticals, each over 1,000,000,000 light years in diameter. These may have grown by galactic cannibalism.

Clusters are gravitationally bound, but there is not enough luminous matter to explain why they have remained gravitationally bound for so long. For example, in the Virgo cluster the speeds with which

The centre of the Virgo Cluster of galaxies, the closest to the Local Group.

the individual galaxies are moving would have broken the cluster up after only a few billion years, much less than the assumed age of the clusters. Clusters must, therefore, contain mass which is not directly visible and which holds them together gravitationally – one example of the existence of 'dark' matter.

The clusters are grouped into superclusters, up to 250,000,000 light years across. The Local Group is on the edge of the Virgo supercluster which contains more than 5,000 galaxies.

Active Galaxies

OBSERVING THE spectra of a galaxy reveals the radiation it is emitting in addition to visible light. Many galaxies emit large amounts of energy at radio, infrared, ultraviolet and X-ray wavelengths.

Irregular starburst galaxies (M82 pictured) produce more radiation from their discs than normal spirals.

Starburst galaxies are spirals that produce extra radiation from their discs, mainly in the infrared. It is thought that the cause is a recent (within the last few million years) spate of star formation, possibly triggered by a close encounter with another galaxy.

ACTIVE GALACTIC NUCLEI

OTHER TYPES of active galaxies are collectively known as active galactic nuclei (AGNs) because it is from within their nuclei that the extra radiation is emitted. One model for AGNs attempts to explain all the phenomena observed.

The key element in the model is a super-massive black hole (far more massive than the end points of some stars). A black hole is so small and massive that its gravitational field is immense: nothing can escape from its vicinity. The boundary from where nothing can escape is called the event horizon. No

Quasar 3C273 with possible black hole at its centre.

The light from this distant quasar (which are remote and very active AGNs) has been split in two by the gravitational effect of a much closer galaxy, making it appear to the viewer to be a twin quasar. The image on the right, shown in false colour is an enlargement from the image on the left.

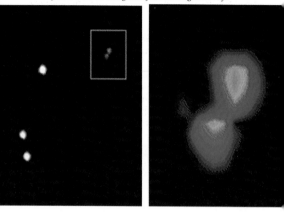

one understands what occurs beyond the event horizon, although speculation is rife, because, where black holes are concerned, our laws of physics break down.

Material approaching a black hole will be pulled towards it, forming an accretion disc which spirals down beyond the event horizon. It is from the accretion disc that the observed energy is emitted. In some AGNs, two jets of radio waves are produced along the poles. Around the accretion disc is a band of dusty material. The different types of active galaxies are explained depending on the observer's view.

Seyfert galaxies are spirals or barred spirals with very bright, compact nuclei. They radiate over a wide range of wavelengths, particularly in the infrared, ultraviolet and X-ray. There are two types of Seyferts: some have broad and narrow emission lines (Type I), others have only narrow lines (Type II).

RADIO GALAXIES

A RADIO galaxy has a compact central source from which jets of radio emissions are emitted. Some radio sources have star-like optical images. These quasi-stellar radio sources, or quasars, are now believed to be remote AGNs. Most quasars lie at vast distances from the Sun, and must be thousands of times more luminous than a conventional galaxy. The abundance of quasars at vast distances suggest they were more prevalent in the early stages of the Universe.

The majority of quasars lie a vast distance from the Sun, such as quasar PKS2349 (pictured), as seen by the Hubble Space Telescope.

UNDERSTANDING THE UNIVERSE

Ancient Beliefs

IF YOU stand in a field away from lights and look up at the night sky, you can see that Earth appears flat and that it sits at the bottom of an upside-down bowl on which the stars are fixed (the celestial sphere). The celestial sphere slowly revolves around Earth, carrying the stars by night and the Sun by day.

This model of a flat Earth at the centre of the Universe held sway in many ancient cultures. The movements of the celestial objects were studied and used as a basis for timekeeping and

It is possible that the pyramids at Giza served as enormous timekeepers by the ancient Egyptians.

navigation. For example the heliacal rising of Sirius (rising before the Sun after being absent from the night sky for 70 days) was used by the Egyptians to warn of the annual flooding of the Nile.

CALENDARS

THE ROMANS based their calendar on the lunar month. The Babylonians based their calendar on the times of the equinoxes (when the Sun crosses the celestial equator and there is equal night and day) and the solstices (when the Sun appears at its highest or lowest in the sky). The times of these events slowly alter, however, because Earth's axis of rotation moves round 360 degrees in about

Some archeologists believe Stonehenge to have been an ancient astronomical observatory built to track the movement of the Sun through the year.

25,800 years. This movement is known as precession. Large monuments like the pyramids and Stonehenge were possibly used as giant timekeepers.

Other events were unpredictable, like the appearance of bright comets or supernovae and the occurrence of lunar and solar eclipses. Ancient astronomers struggled to predict these events, often believing they were portents of doom.

Ancient Greek Astronomy

T HE ANCIENT Greeks had a profound effect on astronomy. Plato (*c.* 427–347 BC) and his pupil Aristotle

(*c.* 384–322 BC) argued that the heavens were perfect and unchanging. Since the circle is the most perfect shape, all heavenly motion must be circular. It was an idea that hindered the progress of astronomy for almost two thousand years.

Ancient Greek men of science like Plato (pictured) and his pupil, Aristotle, argued that the heavens were unchangeable.

THE GRECIAN VIEW

OTHER GREEKS made important contributions on which later astronomers could build. Aristarchus (*c.* 310–230 BC) attempted to measure the size and distance of celestial objects and showed that the Sun was much larger and further away than the Moon. Eratosthenes (*c.* 276–194 BC) measured Earth's circumference and found it to be 40,000 km (25,000 miles). The true figure is 39,940 km (24,819 miles).

Hipparchus (190–120 BC) mapped the positions of over a thousand stars and followed the movement of the five visible planets for more than 30 years. He was also the originator of the magnitude system of measuring the brightness of celestial objects.

Ptolemy (c. AD 100–170) created the *Almagest* – an epic 13 books of astronomical knowledge. His idea of how the planets moved was similar to Aristotle's with Earth at the centre of the celestial sphere that held the 'fixed' stars. The Sun, Moon and planets moved on other spheres, with Earth displaced slightly from their centres, and the planets moved in circular 'epicycles' around their main circle, the 'deferent'.

Ptolemy's method of predicting the movements was very complicated, but it worked, and the *Almagest* endured as an astronomical bible for 14 centuries, although huge errors had crept in by the fifteenth century.

Ptolemy of Alexandria (pictured) produced the Almagest, *an epic masterpiece comprised of 13 books on astronomy.*

Changing Perceptions

COPERNICUS

NICHOLAS COPERNICUS (1473–1543), a Polish Canon, suggested that the planets, including Earth, orbited the Sun. This heliocentric view of the Universe explained why Mercury and Venus are always close to the Sun in the sky as their orbits lie inside that of Earth's. It also explained the retrograde motion of the outer planets – the way they appear to stop and travel backwards as Earth 'undertakes' them.

Copernicus's model still used circular motion and he had to resort to epicycles to make it appear accurate. Copernicus's ideas were published in the year of his death but the book, *De Revolutionibus Orbiun Coelestium* ('On the Revolutions of the Heavenly Orbs'), was difficult to read and only a few understood its message.

Nicholas Copernicus created a model of the Universe which placed the Sun at the centre of all planetary bodies.

TYCHO AND KEPLER

IN 1572, a supernova exploded in the constellation of Cassiopeia. A Danish nobleman, Tycho Brahe (1546–1601), tried to measure its distance from Earth. If Earth is moving around the Sun, the new star should show some slight change against the far away 'fixed' stars (a measurement known as parallax).

Tycho could not discern any movement so assumed that Copernicus's heliocentric universe was wrong. The huge distances between stars meant that he was trying to measure a tiny angle; the first stellar parallax was successfully measured in 1838 by Friedrich Bessel.

Tycho continued to observe for more than 30 years and made an accurate and meticulous study of the movements of the planets. One of Tycho's assistants was Johannes Kepler (1571–1630) who had been born in Germany into a poor Protestant family. Eight years after Tycho's death, Kepler used Tycho's observations to help him compute the orbit of Mars: it moves in an ellipse, with the Sun at one focus.

Kepler published three laws of planetary motion, explaining the motion of the planets in a simple manner without recourse to epicycles.

Tycho Brahe, the Danish astronomer, upon whose work Kepler was later to base his calculations.

GALILEO

GALILEO GALILEI (1564–1642) was one of the first to use a telescope for astronomy. His observations confirmed Kepler's ideas. Galileo saw the phases of Mercury and Venus, caused because they are between the Earth and Sun. He saw the four brightest moons of Jupiter orbiting a body other than Earth and obeying Kepler's laws. Galileo's observations helped to move Earth from the centre of the Universe.

Galileo Galilei, the Italian astronomer and physicist, one of the greatest scientists of all time.

NEWTON

ON CHRISTMAS DAY, less than a year after Galileo died, Isaac Newton (1642–1727) was born. When Cambridge University was closed because of the plague, Newton worked from his home in Woolsthorpe, where he developed his three laws of universal motion. He introduced the concept of gravity, a force that exists between all bodies, and he showed that Kepler's laws followed logically from his deductions. His famous *Principia Mathematica*, explained the mechanics of the Solar System in mathematical terms.

Applying his gravitational theory to the stars, Newton argued that the Universe must be infinite with the stars scattered throughout, otherwise the force of gravity would pull them all together. This led to a paradox popularised by Heinrich Olbers: 'Why is the sky dark at night?'

If the Universe is infinite, starlight would reach Earth from every direction; there would be no dark, starless areas. To overcome this paradox, it was suggested that the Universe had not existed forever so the light from some stars had not had time to reach Earth.

Isaac Newton's profoundly influential Principia Mathematica *was published in 1687.*

EINSTEIN

NEWTONIAN MECHANICS works well for most objects, but where gravity is strong or bodies are moving at, or near, the speed of light, errors creep in.

Albert Einstein (1879–1955) formulated his general theory of relativity in which the mass of an object alters the shape of space and the flow of time around it. Einstein tested his theory by correctly calculating a small discrepancy in the motion of the planet Mercury, a discrepancy that astronomers had long been unable to explain.

When Einstein applied his theories to the Universe, his mathematics showed it was either expanding or contracting.

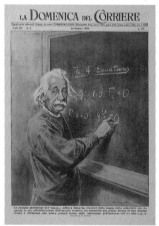

Even in the early twentieth century Einstein was still influenced by Aristotelian beliefs that the 'perfect' heavens should be unchanging, and he introduced a cosmological constant into the theory to make it work for a static Universe.

Albert Einstein (1879–1955), founder of the theory of relativity, teaching at Princeton University in 1950.

AN EXPANDING UNIVERSE

EDWIN HUBBLE (1889–1953) observed the spectra of spiral galaxies and discovered that they were moving away from us. The farther the galaxy, the faster it moved. This is Hubble's Law and the constant that relates the distance to the speed of a galaxy is the Hubble constant (H_O).

As everything in the Universe is moving away from everything else, in the past, everything was closer together. At the very beginning, everything in the Universe was packed into an infinitesimal space which exploded apart. This event is called the Big Bang.

Edwin Hubble (1889–1953), the US astronomer after whom the revolutionary Hubble Space Telescope was named.

A Russian scientist, George Gamow (1904–68), proposed that the Universe was incredibly hot at the time of the Big Bang. As the Universe expanded, the radiation cooled, until it would now have a temperature of around 3K (-270°C/-460°F). This cosmic background radiation was discovered in 1965 by two telephone engineers, Arno Penzias and Robert Wilson.

The Big Bang

THE UNIVERSE is everything; all matter, radiation and time came into being at the Big Bang. It is meaningless to ask what happened before the Big Bang, or what lies outside the Universe.

Before the Planck time (10^{-43} seconds), our laws of physics break down. At the Planck time, the temperature was immense and radiation would have been extremely high-energy gamma rays. As the Universe expanded, the radiation cooled, losing energy, allowing different events to occur.

During the inflationary period at 10^{-35} seconds, the Universe expanded at a huge rate, explaining why the Universe generally looks the same in all directions.

Max Karl Ernst Ludwig Planck (1858–1947), German physicist and 1918 Nobel Prize winner.

Russian atomic expert and astrophysicist, George Gamow (right), explained how the Universe was unbelievably hot at the onset of the Big Bang.

The Big Bang; Essential Data

Time	Mean Temperature Radiation of Universe	Event
Less than 10^{-43} seconds (Planck time)	10^{30} K	Our laws of physics break down
Greater than 10^{-43} seconds	10^{30} K	Collisions between gamma rays produce particles and antimatter. Antimatter differs from matter only by its charge.
10^{35} seconds		Inflationary period when space expands at an incredible rate.
About one second	6×10^{9} K	Energy of gamma rays falls to less than that required to create particles and anti-particles. A slight excess of matter.
About 3 minutes		Gamma rays can no longer stop protons and neutrons combining to form the nuclei of helium and deuterium (heavy hydrogen). The predicted ratio of helium to hydrogen created is observed in the oldest stars.
About 1,000,000 years	About 3,000K (2,727°C/4,940°F)	Electrons and nuclei no longer have enough energy to overcome the electromagnetic attraction between them and they start to form atoms. Space becomes transparent to radiation.
About 500,000,000 years		Formation of galaxies begins.
About 20,000,000,000 years	About 3K (-270°C/-460°F)	You read this book

How It All Works

THE NATURE OF LIGHT

LIGHT IS radiation. Radiation stretches across the whole of the electromagnetic (em) spectrum from the low-energy (long wavelength) radio waves to the high-energy (short wavelength) gamma rays. Visible light is just a small part of the em spectrum; special only in that our eyes respond to it because the Sun emits most of its radiation in this part of the em spectrum.

Radiation can be thought of as tiny packets of energy called photons which travel as waves. The higher the energy of the radiation, the higher the energy of the photons and the shorter the wavelength.

In 1865, the Scottish physicist, James Clerk Maxwell (1831–79), showed that electric and magnetic forces are two aspects of the same phenomenon: electromagnetism. All radiation travels through empty space at a speed of 299,792.458 km/s

The Scottish physicist, James Clerk Maxwell, who explained the phenomenon we now know as electromagnetism.

Sir Isaac Newton demonstrated that white light could be split into a spectrum of separate colours.

(186,300 mps). If an object is one light year away, the radiation (or light) takes one year travelling at this speed to reach us. One light year is 9.4605×10^{12} km (5.86×10^{12} miles).

Radiation from objects farther away takes longer to reach us, so the farther away we observe, the farther back in time we see. The Andromeda Galaxy is about 2,250,000 million light years away, so we see it as it was 2,250,000 million years ago. The furthest we can see is about 15,000,000,000 light years.

Isaac Newton showed that white light can be split into a spectrum of colours with red light having a longer wavelength than blue. In 1814, a German physicist, Joseph Fraunhofer (1787–1826), discovered that the solar spectrum has hundreds of dark and bright lines crossing it. These lines are the fingerprints of different elements.

INSIDE ATOMS

IN 1910, a New Zealand physicist, Ernest Rutherford (1871–1937), concluded that the mass of an atom is concentrated in the positively charged nucleus which has negatively charged electrons in orbit about it. The simplest atom (hydrogen) consists of one proton and one electron.

Other atoms also have particles with no electric charge (neutrons) in their nuclei.

Electrons exist in specific orbits depending on their energy. If an atom is heated, electrons gaining energy jump to higher energy orbits, or leave orbit entirely. In the latter case, the atom becomes ionised. If an electron loses energy, it drops back to a lower orbit.

As an electron changes orbit, it emits or absorbs a photon.

Ernest Rutherford discovered the atom.

This causes the lines across a spectrum; bright emission lines occur when photons are emitted, dark absorption lines occur when a photon is absorbed.

Each element has a distinct set of lines, so analysis of spectra can tell scientists the chemical composition of an object as well as its temperature.

MOVING LINES

WHEN SOME objects are observed, the spectral lines are shifted from their expected position. In 1842, an Austrian mathematician, Christian Doppler (1803–53), explained how the movement of an object can change the wavelength of emitted radiation.

If objects are moving apart, the wavelengths become stretched (redshifted); if they are moving towards each other, the wavelengths become squashed (blueshifted). Normally, in astronomy, they are redshifted (moved towards the red part of the em spectrum). This Doppler shift is a powerful tool in astronomy.

Emission line spectra for an assortment of chemical elements: from these spectra it is possible for scientists to gather a great deal of information about each element.

THE FUTURE OF THE UNIVERSE

The Expanding Universe

THE FATE of the Universe depends upon its mean density. If the density of matter within the Universe is low, the associated gravitational field will be too small to stop the Universe expanding infinitely. This is called an open universe, where if parallel lines travelled far enough, they would eventually diverge. In such a universe, the galaxies would get farther and farther apart, and the Universe would continue to cool. Star formation would cease and the Universe would become cold and dark.

If the density of matter is high, the associated gravitational field would eventually stop the Universe expanding. The Universe would expand to a finite size, stop and slowly start to contract. The galaxies would start to approach each other and the temperature would rise, until everything reverted back to a cosmic soup of matter and radiation ending in a 'Big Crunch'. This is a closed universe where two parallel lines eventually meet.

Between these two scenarios lies the flat universe where the density of matter is exactly equal to the critical density that will halt expansion. The Universe will continue to expand forever but the

This COBE satellite microwave image shows us the remnants of the radiation produced in the Big Bang.

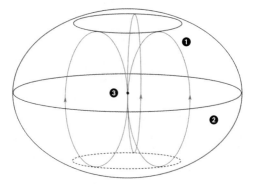

It is possible for the Universe to expand and contract in a series of endless cycles: a theoretical representation of three are shown here, starting at the point of the Big Bang , ❸, expanding in space, ❷, over time, ❶, then folding back , ❸, in a big crunch.

speed of expansion will get slower and slower. The flat universe would suffer the same fate as the open universe, although on a much longer timescale. In the flat universe, parallel lines never meet.

The value of the critical density depends on the rate at which the Universe is expanding, i.e. the Hubble constant. The faster the Universe expands, the more gravitational energy (and hence more matter) is needed to stop it. H_0 is a value difficult to assess because of the errors involved in measuring distances. A value of H_0 between 50 and 75 km/second/Mpc (kilometre per second per megaparsec) gives a critical density between 5×10^{25} and 11×10^{25} times that of water.

DARK MATTER

IF ALL the matter in the Universe consisted of luminous matter, then the mean density of the Universe could be estimated and its fate understood. Unfortunately about 90

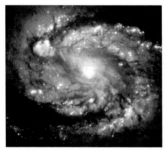

per cent of matter cannot be observed directly. This 'dark matter' is known to exist in clusters of galaxies, keeping them gravitationally bound, and around spiral galaxies, making the luminous outer material orbit more rapidly than it should.

Dark matter exists in spiral galaxies, causing the luminous outer matter to orbit more rapidly than it should.

The nature of this dark matter is unknown. Some of it could be black holes, dim stars or Jupiter-sized planets, all matter that we find difficult to observe with today's technology. Much of it could be non-baryonic matter – matter composed differently to 'ordinary' protons and neutrons. Suggestions include weakly interacting massive particles (WIMPs) and neutrinos with mass.

THE FLATNESS PROBLEM

AMAZINGLY, OBSERVATIONS do point to the Universe being flat. The ratio of the actual mean density to the critical density is denoted by the Greek letter omega (Ω). If the mean density equals the critical density, then omega equals 1. It seems omega deviates from 1 by less than 10 per cent.

As the deviation from 1 is so small, it means that it was even closer to 1 before the inflationary period. Any slight deviation would have been accentuated enormously by the inflation of the Universe.

Dark matter keeps clusters of galaxies (pictured) gravitationally bound.

Unanswered Questions

THERE ARE many questions left unanswered in astronomy. Our theories of objects in the Universe allow us to describe objects we have never actually observed, like black holes. It is impossible to 'see' a black hole, but we can theorise that they exist because of their effect on nearby space.

What happens within a black hole? Our physics breaks down beyond the event horizon, and everything becomes conjecture. Some theorists have suggested there may be a 'worm hole' which will lead to other universes, but so far this is a purely fictional idea. A worm hole would not be able to be used for human travel because anyone approaching the black hole would be torn

We are still on the look-out for signs of other life forms within our Universe.

apart by immense gravitational forces long before the event horizon was reached.

Will it ever be possible to roam the Galaxy at speeds close to the speed of light? If we do not find another method of travel, the vast distances between stars will preclude humankind of exploring much beyond the Solar System.

An artist's impression of how a human colony on Mars may look, although as yet there is no scheduled date for a landing there.

Is there intelligent life elsewhere in the Universe? With the billions of stars just within our own galaxy, statistically there must be, but will we ever make contact? There are programmes in existence like the SETI (Search for Extraterrestrial Intelligence) which are looking for intelligent signals from space, but the chances of discovering a message must be very slim.

The anthropic principle states that the Universe is how it is because we are here to observe it. If the Universe were even slightly different, we may never have existed. Whatever the answers, the Universe is a fascinating place to study.

COMPENDIUM

Glossary

Absolute magnitude: The brightness of an object on the magnitude scale at a standard distance of 10 parsecs (32.6 light years).

Accretion disc: A disc of material spiralling on to an object like a black hole.

Active galactic nuclei (AGN): Compact core of an active galaxy.

Albedo: A measure of the reflectivity of an object: 0 is totally black, 1 is totally reflecting.

Aphelion: The point in an object's orbit furthest from the Sun.

Apparent magnitude: The apparent brightness of an object on the magnitude scale as seen from Earth.

Astronomical unit (AU): The mean distance of Earth from the Sun: 149,597,870 km (92,955,630 miles).

Big Bang: The beginning of the Universe.

Binary star: Two stars gravitationally bound together.

Black hole: An object so dense that its gravitational field can stop any form of radiation escaping.

Celestial equator: A line where Earth's equator would cut the celestial sphere if extended outwards.

Constellation: A named pattern of stars.

Cosmology: Study of the nature and origins of the Universe.

Dark matter: Matter unobservable by ordinary methods.

Density: The mass of an object per unit volume.

Doppler effect: The apparent change in wavelength of an object moving with respect to the observer.

Eccentricity: The extent to which the orbit of an object varies from a circle.

Ecliptic: The plane of Earth's orbit around the Sun and the observed path of the Sun in the sky.

Ejecta: Material thrown out during the creation of an impact crater or basin.

Electromagnetic (em) radiation: Oscillating perpendicular waves of electricity and magnetism.

Electromagnetic spectrum: The full range of electromagnetic radiation arranged according to wavelength.

Equinoxes: Dates when the Sun passes through the celestial equator (21 March and 23 September).

Galaxy: Giant systems containing stars, gas and dust.

Gas giants: The four large, mainly gas, planets in the outer Solar System (Jupiter, Saturn, Uranus and Neptune).

Gravitational field: The region of space surrounding a body where its gravity has an effect on other bodies.

Hertzsprung-Russell diagram: A diagram showing the positions of the stars according to their luminosity and surface temperature.

Hubble's constant: The parameter connecting the rate at which the Universe expands with distance.

Interstellar clouds: Denser regions in the material lying between the stars.

Interstellar medium: Matter lying between the stars.

Lagrangian point: Places where the gravitational field of objects combine in such a way that smaller objects can sometimes remain in stable orbit about them.

Light year: The distance travelled by light or any other form of radiation through a vacuum in one year: 9.46×10^{12} km (5.86×10^{12} miles).

Limb: The edge of the visible disc of an object.

Local Group: The small group of galaxies to which the Milky Way belongs.

Luminosity: The total amount of energy radiated by a star per second.

Magnetic field: A field of force around an object containing some form of magnet.

Magnetotail: The region of a planet's magnetic field on the side opposite the Sun pulled out by the solar wind.

Main sequence: The region on the Hertzsprung-Russell diagram where stars are changing hydrogen to helium in their cores by nuclear fusion.

Messier numbers: The numbers of objects in Charles Messier's catalogue of non-cometary nebulous objects.

Mass: A measure of the amount of material within a body.

Milky Way: The faint band of light visible across the night-sky from the stars in the Galactic plane and the name of the galaxy to which the Solar System belongs.

Neutron star: The end point of a star stopped from collapsing by the force between neutrons.

Orbit: The path of one celestial object around another.

Parallax: The apparent shift due to the movement of the observer of an object's position against objects further away.

Perihelion: The point in an object's orbit nearest to the Sun.

Planet: A body that orbits a star and shines by reflected starlight.

Planetary nebula: An expanding cloud of stellar material ejected by a star evolving off the main sequence.

Population I: Young, metal-rich stars.

Population II: Old, metal-poor stars.

Precession: The slow movement of Earth's axis of rotation.

Proper motion: The movement of a star across the sky (expressed in angular measurement).

Pulsar: A rotating neutron star.

Quasar: A very bright, distant object thought to be a type of active galactic nucleus.

Redshift: The movement of spectral lines towards the red part (longer wavelength) of the em spectrum due to an object's relative motion away from the observer.

Separation: The angular distance between two components of a visual binary or an optical double star.

Solar System: The Sun and all objects which orbit the Sun including Earth.

Solar wind: The constant flow of material (composed mainly of electrons and protons) from the Sun.

Solstices: Dates at which the Sun reaches its highest or lowest point in the sky (21 June and 21 December).

Spectral lines: Bright or dark lines in a spectrum indicating the emission or absorption of photons.

Star: A gaseous body that shines due to its own internal energy source.

Supernova: A cataclysmic explosion of a star.

Terminator: The line between day and night on a planet or moon.

Terrestrial planets: The four rocky, inner planets of the inner Solar System (Mercury, Venus, Earth and Mars).

Variable stars: Stars whose brightness changes over relatively short periods of time.

White dwarf: The end point of a star stopped collapsing by the force between electrons.

Further Reading & Useful Addresses

Illingworth, Valerie, (ed.),
Collins Dictionary of Astronomy,
HarperCollins (new ed. 2000)

Kaufmann, William J., II,
Universe, W. H. Freeman and
Company (1998)

Levy, David, *Skywatching,*
HarperCollins (1995)

Nicolson, Iain, *Unfolding Our
Universe,* Cambridge
University Press (1999)

Ridpath, Ian, *Collins Gem Stars,*
HarperCollins (2000)

Ridpath, Ian, *Stars and Planets,*
Harper Collins (1993)

Spence, Pam (ed.), *The Universe
Revealed,* Mitchell Beazley
(1998)

Stott, Carole, *New Astronomer,*
Dorling Kindersley (1999)

USEFUL ADDRESSES

**British Astronomical
Association**
Burlington House, Piccadilly,
London WIV 9AG, UK
http://www.ast.cam.ac.uk/~baa

European Space Agency (ESA)
8–10 rue Mario Nikis, 75738
Paris Cedex 15, France
http://www.esa.int

**Federation of Astronomical
Societies (UK)**
10, Glan-y-Llyn, North Cornelly,
Bridgend CF33 4EF, UK
Secretary: Clive Down
http://www.fedastro.org.uk

**National Aeronautics and Space
Administration (NASA)**
Office of Human Resources
and Education
Education Division, Mail Code
FE, NASA Headquarters,
Washington,
DC 20546-0001, USA
http://www.nasa.gov

**Particle Physics and Astronomy
Research Council (PPARC)**
Polaris House, North Star
Avenue, Swindon SN2 1SZ, UK
http://www.pparc.ac.uk

Royal Astronomical Society
Burlington House, Piccadilly,
London WIV ONL, UK
http://www.ras.org.uk

Space Science Institute
Office of Public Outreach
3700 Sam Martin Drive, Johns
Hopkins University, Baltimore
MD 21218, USA
http://www.stsci.edu/top.html

Society For Popular Astronomy
36 Fairway, Keyworth,
Nottingham, NG12 5DU, UK
Secretary: Guy Fennimore
http://popastro.com

PICTURE CREDITS

Mary Evans Picture Library:
108, 109, 165, 166, 168, 170
(left), 171 (right), 172, 173
Foundry Arts: 12, 13, 54, 73, 74,
78, 119, 125, 133, 150, 177

Galaxy Pictures/Robin Scagell:
3 (far left; far right), 6, 7, 10, 11,
15, 17, 18, 19, 20, 21, 22, 24,
25, 26, 27, 29, 30, 31, 32, 33,
34, 36, 37, 38, 39, 40, 41, 42,
44, 45, 46, 47, 48, 50, 51, 52,
53, 56, 57, 58, 60, 61, 62, 64,
65, 66, 67, 68, 69, 72, 75, 76,
79, 80, 82, 83, 84, 85, 86, 88,
89, 90, 91, 92, 94, 95, 96, 97,
98, 99, 101, 102, 103, 104, 105,
106, 107, 110, 112, 113, 114,
116, 117, 121, 122, 123, 124,
126, 127, 128, 129, 136, 137,
138, 139, 141, 143, 145, 146,
147, 148, 149, 151, 152, 153,
154, 155, 156, 157, 158, 159,
176, 178, 179, 181

Photodisc: 134

Popperfoto: 111

**Science and Society Picture
Library:** 28, 93, 100, 140, 144,
163, 175

Science Photo Library: 169

Topham Picturepoint: 3
(middle left; middle right), 14,
70, 81, 131, 160, 161, 162, 164,
173, 180

ACKNOWLEDGEMENTS
With grateful thanks to Anna
Amari, Philip Hempnell, Cathy
Lowne and Colin Rudderham for
all their help.

Index

achondrites *def* 111, 113
Adrastes (moon of Jupiter) 48
AGNs (active galactic nuclei) see under galaxies
Aldrin, Buzz *94*, 95
Algol 140
Almagest, the 163
Amalthea (moon of Jupiter) 48
Amor asteroids 100, 103
Ananke (moon of Jupiter) 48
Andromeda Galaxy *143*, 154, 173
Antennae Galaxy 151
Apollo asteroids 100, 103
Apollo space programme 94-5, *94-5*
Aren asteroids 100
Ariel (moon of Uranus) *61*
Aristarchus 162
Aristotle 162-3, 168
Armstrong, Neil *94*, 95
asteroid 2060 see Chiron asteroid
asteroids 11, 16, 89, 96-103, *98-103*, 99, 111, 113
near-earth objects (NEOs) 100
orbits 47, 98
origin 98, 103
see also individual asteroids
astronomical units (AU) *def* 16
Aten asteroids 100, 103
Atlas (moon of Saturn) 57
atoms 174

AU *see* astronomical units

Babylon 160
Barnard's star 127
Beehive Cluster 147, *147*
Bessel, Friedrich 165
Betelgeuse 127
'Big Bang' 152, 169-70, *171*
'Big Crunch' 176
binary stars 140-1
black holes 136, 149, *149*, 157, 178, 180
blazars 159
Bopp, Thomas *107-8*
Brahe, Tycho 165, *165*
Burney, Venetia 15

calendars 160
Callisto (moon of Jupiter) 48-9
Caloris Basin (Mercury) 27
Canis Major constellation *128*
Canis Minor constellation *128*
Capricorn constellation *129*
Carme (moon of Jupiter) 48
Cartwheel Galaxy 151
'Cassini division' 54, *54*
Cassini probe 57
cataclysmic variable stars 141
centaurs 100, *101*, 103
Cepheid variable stars 139, 144
Ceres (meteoroid) 16, 16
Cetus constellation 139
Chandrasekhar limit 136

Charon (moon of Pluto) 11, 19, 21, 68, *68*, 68-9
Chicxulub crater 76
Chiron asteroid 100, *101*, 103, *103*
chondrites *def* 111
Christy, James 68
Clementine probes 95
clusters 147, 154-5, *155*
globular clusters 139, 147, 149
gravitational attraction 155
superclusters 154-5
comae 103, 105, 107
comets 14, 16-18, 100, 102-9, *103-9*, 142, 161
formation of 11, 16-18, 97
long-period 17-18, 104, 108
missions to 109
orbits 16-18, 100, 104-5, 108
short-period 18, 104, 108
tails 16, 104, 106-7, *106-7*
see also Hale-Bopp comet, Halley's comet
constellations *126-9*, 129
Copernicus, Nicholas 164-5
Cordelia (moon of Uranus) 60
Corona Borealis 141
coronal mass ejections (CMEs) 123
cosmic spherules 110
Crab Nebula *146*, 147

dark matter 146-7, 155, 178, *178-9*
d'Arrest, H 14
Deimos (moon of Mars) 40-1, 41, *41*
Delta Cephei 139
Despina (moon of Neptune) 65
Dione (moon of Saturn) 57
Doppler, Christian 175
Dreyer, JLE 142
dust, interstellar 16, 96, 103, 106-7, 110, 113-14, 141, 145-9

Earth 6, *6*, 11-12, 14, *20*, *70*, 70-81, 71, *72-6*, *78-81*, 90-5, 159, 163
  atmosphere 77-81, *78-9*
  formation of 72
  life on 21, 70, 80-1, *80-1*
  magnetic field 79
  orbit 16, 71, 78-9, 124-5, 127, 162, 164-5
  rotation 78-9, 89
  structure and surface 21, 71-6, *72-6*
  water 21, 70, 77-8, 79, 80, 90, *92*, 93
  see also gravitational influence under Moon
ecliptic plane *see under* Earth
Egypt, ancient 160
Einstein, Albert 168, *168*
Elara (moon of Jupiter) 48
electromagnetism 172-3
Enceladus (moon of Saturn) 54-5, 57
Eratosthenes 162
Eros asteroid *102*

Europa (moon of Jupiter) 6, 48-9
event horizons 157

Fraunhofer, Joseph 173

Galatea (moon of Neptune) 65
galaxies 7, 142-59, *143-59*, 176
  active galaxies 156-9
    active galactic nuclei (AGNs) 157-9
  discovery of 142-4
  elliptical 150, *150*, 152, 155
  formation of 149, 152-3
  irregular galaxies 150-1
  lenticular galaxies 150-1
  protogalaxies 152-3
  radio galaxies 158-9
  Seyfert galaxies 157-8, *158*
  spiral galaxies 148, 150-3, *151*, 156-7, 169, 178
  starburst galaxies 156
  structure 154-5
Galilei, Galileo 166, *166*
Galileo probe 46, 48
Galle, JG 14
Gamow, George 169, *170*
Ganymede (moon of Jupiter) 48-9, 49
gas, interstellar 16, 96, 103, 105, 110, 114, 145-6, 148-9, 152
Gemini constellation *126*
Giotto probe 109
gravitational forces 11, 17-19, 166, 168, *179*
  see also under individual planets
Greece, ancient 162-3

Hale, Alan 107, 108
Hale-Bopp comet 7, *107*, 107-8
Hall, Asaph 40
Halley, Edmund *108*, 109
Halley's comet 18, 105, 108-9, *109*
Hercules constellation 147
Herschel, John 142
Herschel, William 14, *14*, 58, 142
Hertzsprung-Russell diagram *132*, 132-5
Hertzsprung, Ejnar 132
Himalia (moon of Jupiter) 48
Hipparchus 162
Hirayama families 99
Horsehead Nebula *117*, 146-7
Hubble, Edwin 144, 150, 152, 169, *169*
  Hubble Constant 169, 177
  Hubble Space Telescope 147
Huygens, Christian 56
Huygens probe 57

Iaperus (moon of Saturn) 57
Icarus asteroid 100
impact ejecta 111
Io (moon of Jupiter) 46, 48-9, *49*
Jewitt, David 19
Jupiter 11, *13*, 13-14, *20*, 20-1, 42-9, *42-9*, 43
  atmosphere 42-4, 50-2, 58, 63-4
  gravitational attraction 46-7, 47, 100, 108
  Great Red Spot 44-5, 45, 52
  magnetism 46-7
  missions to 44

moons 6, 11, 21, 43, 46, 48-9, *48-9*, 49, 166
see also individual moons
orbit 16, 20-1, 52, 100, 105
Lagrangian points 100
rings 44, *44*
rotation 43-4, 52
structure and surface 12, 21, 42-6, *46*

Kepler, Johannes 21, 165-6
Kirkwood gaps 98
Kowal-Meech-Belton comet see Chiron asteroid
Kuiper belt *def* 17, 11-12, 18-19, *19*, 65-7, 97, 100, 102, 104

Le Verrier, Urbain 14
Leda (moon of Jupiter) 48
life, extra-terrestrial 36, 81, 181
see also under Earth
light 13, 114, 119-20, 121, 129-31, *130*, 156, 162, 166-7, 172-3
speed of 7, 168, 173, 180
see also starlight *under* stars
Lowell Observatory 15
Lowell, Percival 15, *15*
Luna 3 probe 87
Luu, Jane 19
Lyra 147
Lysithea (moon of Jupiter) 48

Magellan probe 33
Magellanic Clouds 151, 154-5
Mariner probes 33, 39

Mariner 10 probe 26, 33
Mars *11*, 12-13, *13*, 20, 34-41, *34-41*, 35, 111
atmosphere 12, 35-6, 38-9
magnetic field 34, 39
missions to 36-7, 39, 181
moons 11, 39-41, 40-1
see also individual moons
observation of 13, 34
orbit 11, 16, 20-1, 34-5, 35, 100, 165
rotation 34, 35
structure and surface 21, 34-9, *36-9*, 75
canals 36
Mars Global Surveyor probe 36-7, 39
Maxwell, James Clerk 172, *172*
Mercury 11-13, *13*, 20, 20-7, *22-7*, 23
atmosphere 23
gravity 27
magnetic field 22-3
orbit 11, 20-1, 22-3, 23, *24*, 25, 164, 166, 168
rotation 22, 23, 25
structure and surface 21-7, *25-6*
Messier, Charles 142
Messier Catalogue 142, 145, 147, 149
Meteor Crater 76, 76
meteorites 110-13, *110-13*, 113
composition of 111-13
meteoroids 16, 16, 26-7
meteors 110, 113
Metis (moon of Jupiter) 48
Milky Way Galaxy 7, 81, 144-5, 148-9, *148-9*, *154*, 154-5

galactic centre 149, *149*
Local Group *154*, 154-5
Mimas (moon of Saturn) 57
Mira *138*, 139
Miranda (moon of Uranus) *60*
Moon, the 11, 21, 82, *82-3*, 82-95, *85-95*, 111, 124
atmosphere 94
axis of rotation 82, 87, 89
formation of 89
gravitational influence 90, *92*, 93
lunar eclipses 93, 160
lunar phases 90-1, *91*
magnetic field 83
missions to 84, 87, 94-5, *94-5*
orbit round Earth 82, 82, 89-91, 124-5, 162-3
structure and surface 26, 83-8, 94-5, *94-5*

Naiad (moon of Neptune) 65
navigation 160
near-earth objects (NEOs) 100-1, 103
nebulae *137*, 144-7, *145-7*
dark nebulae 146-7
emission nebulae 145-6
planetary nebulae *def* 135, 147
reflection nebulae 147
see also individual nebulae
Neptune 13-14, *20*, 62, 62-5, *62-5*, 102
atmosphere 63
gravitational attraction 19
Great Dark Spot 63

magnetic field 63
missions to 63, 65
moons 11, 19, 21, 64-5
  see also individual moons
orbit 11, 62, 66, 97
rings *64*, 65
rotation 62, 63-4
structure and surface 12, 21, 58, 62, *63*, 63-4

Nereid (moon of Neptune) 65
neutron stars *see under* stars

New General Catalogue 142, 144
Newton, Sir Isaac 166-7, 173, *173*
non-baryonic matter 178
novae 141
nuclear fusion 116, 133, 135

Olbers, Heinrich 166-7
Oort, JH 17
Oort cloud 11, 13 16-17, 97, 104, 108
Ophelia (moon of Uranus) 60
Orion Nebula *128*, 129, 145, *145*, 146

Pan (moon of Saturn) 57
Pandora (moon of Saturn) 55
Pasiphae (moon of Jupiter) 48
Pathfinder probe 39
Penzias, Arno 169, *169*
Perseus constellation *127*, 140
Phaethon asteroid 100
Phobos 2 probe 39
Phobos (moon of Mars) 39-41, *40*, 41

Phoebe (moon of Saturn) 57
Pioneer II probe 55
Planck, Max 170, *170*
'Planet X' 15
planetoids see asteroids
planets *12-13*, 12-15, 20-81, 162
ecliptic plane *def* 34, 60, 69, 124
gas giants *see* Jupiter, Neptune, Saturn, Uranus
laws of planetary motion 21, 165-6
orbits 11, 16, 20-1, 163-4
terrestrial planets *see* Earth, Mars, Mercury, Venus
  see also individual planets
Plato 162
Pleiades 147
Pluto 13, *20*, 21, 65-9, *66-9*, 67
discovery of 15
moon *see* Charon
orbit 11-12, 66
origin of 12, 66-7
rotation 67
structure and surface 12, 21, 66-7, *67*, 67
Polaris (Pole Star) 127
Praesepe *see* Beehive Cluster
Prometheus (moon of Saturn) 55
protostars 134-5, 145
Proxima Centauri 126
Ptolemy 163, *163*
pulsars *def* 136, 147

quasars *157*, 158-9, *159*

R Coronae Borealis stars 141
radio waves 149, 156-9, 172
rainbows 130, *130*

red giants *see under* stars
Rhea (moon of Saturn) 57
Ring Nebula 147
Rome, ancient 160
Rosse, Lord 134
RR Lyrae stars 139
Russell, Henry Norris 132
Rutherford, Ernest 174, *174*

S/1999JI (moon of Jupiter) 48
Sagittarius constellation 149
Saturn 13, *13*, *20*, 50-7, *50-7*, 51
atmosphere 51-2, *52*, 63-4
magnetic field 52
missions to 54-5, 57
moons 11, 21, 54-7, 56, *56-7*
  see also individual moons
orbit 11, 14, 20-1
rings *21*, 50, 52-5, 52-5, *53*, 57
rotation 51, 52
structure and surface 12, 21, 50-2, 58
Saturn V launch vehicles 95
semiregular variable stars 138, *138*
SETI (Search for Extra-Terrestrial Intelligence) 181
Shoemaker-Levy comet 46
shooting stars *see* meteors
Sinope (moon of Jupiter) 48
Sirius 131
Sirius B 131
Sojourner rover 39

Solar System, the 10-11, 142
  formation of 11-12, 97, 112
  orbital plane 16
solar wind 79, 123
space debris 6, 16, 96-7, 96-7, 110, 113
  see also dust, gas
stars 114-16, 126-41, 126-41, 181
  death of 115-17, 133, 136, 136-7, 149
  eruptive stars 140
  formation of 114-16, 132, 134-5, 145, 149, 156
  gravitational attraction 115, 118, 136, 140, 151
  main-sequence stars 116, 134-5, 147
  mapping 58, 142, 145, 147, 149
  neutron stars 136
  pulsating stars 138, 138-9
  red giants 132, 133, 135, 139
  starlight 129, 130-3, 132, 138-41, 138-41, 146-9, 153, 166-7
  supergiants 127, 132, 133, 135, 139, 141
  variable stars 138, 138-41
Stonehenge 160, 160
Sun, the 6-7, 7, 10, 12-13, 16-18, 25, 30, 46, 63, 90, 98, 103-4, 107, 113-26, 115, 140, 140, 142, 148, 163, 165
  birth of 115-16
  as centre of the Universe 164, 164-6
  death of 117
  flares and explosive events on 120, 123, 123, 140

gravitational influence 11, 47, 93, 100, 105
magnetic field 121-3
radiation and light 132, 132-3, 172
solar eclipses 124-5, 124-5, 160
solar neutrinos 120, 121
structure 118-23
sunspots 121-3, 122
  see also solar wind
superclusters *see under* clusters
supergiants *see under* stars
supernovae 115, 147, 160
Surveyor 3 95

T Tauri stars 141
Taurus constellation 141, 141
telescopes 13, 66, 126-7, 135, 144-5
Tethys (moon of Saturn) 57
Thalassa (moon of Neptune) 65
Thebe (moon of Jupiter) 48
Titan (moon of Saturn) 56-7
Tombaugh, Clyde W 15, 69
Trapezium 145
Triangulum Galaxy 154
Trifid Nebula 117
Triton (moon of Neptune) 12, 19, 64, 65-6
Trojan asteroids 100

Universe, the *def* 6, *def* 170, 7, 159
  contraction of 168
  expansion of 168-9, 176-9
  flat 176-9
  future of 176-9

Uranus 13, 20, 58-61, 58-61, 69
  atmosphere 58
  axis and rotation 29, 29, 60, 69
  discovery of 14, 58
  magnetic field 60
  mission to 60
  moons 11, 21, 60, 60-1, 61
    see also individual moons
  orbit 11, 14, 60, 69
  rings 60
  structure and surface 12, 21, 58, 63
  UV Ceti variable stars 140

Van Allen belts 79
Venera probes 33
Venus 11-13, 13, 14, 20, 28-33, 28-33, 69
  atmosphere 6, 21, 28
  missions to 30, 33
  orbit 20-1, 28, 29, 164, 166
  rotation 28-9
  structure and surface 6, 21, 28-33, 31-3, 75
Viking probes 39, 41
Virgo Cluster 155, 155
Voyager probes 11, 44-5, 54-5, 60, 63, 65

W Virginia stars 139
water 21, 25, 35-6, 49, 52, 58, 66, 70, 78, 79, 80
  see also under Earth
white dwarves 117, 131, 132, 133, 136, 137, 141
Wilson, Robert 169
WIMPs (Weakly Interacting Massive Particles) 178
worm holes 180